PROVIDENCE

PROVIDENCE

Michael J. Langford

SCM PRESS LTD

334 01342 9

First published 1981
by SCM Press Ltd
58 Bloomsbury Street London WC1

Phototypeset by Input Typesetting Ltd
and printed in Great Britain by
Richard Clay Ltd (The Chaucer Press)
Bungay

Acknowledgment

I am grateful to Dr Peter Baelz, Dean of Durham, for many valuable suggestions during the preparation of this book.

Contents

I

Introduction

1. The aim of the book

'Providence' is one of our concepts that needs clarification. A brief definition will be offered, but this will raise many problems that require careful analysis. Such analysis will be of value because it reveals a core of meaning in the light of which we can attempt to assess its contemporary value. Further, those who find the concept personally significant, as will most who call themselves Christians or Jews or Muslims, will discover several important implications for their faith. Thus clarity is not my only purpose. It is my initial purpose, but I am also concerned to understand one of the fundamental concepts of Western religion and its implications for life.

Another way of describing my principal aim is to say that it is an exploration of the *grammar* of providence. When we learn a new language, a large part of what is involved consists of learning the complex rules by which words are related to one another. One indication that we understand a word is that we can use it correctly, according to the grammatical rules of a particular language. Similarly, many important concepts, such as 'mind', 'space', and 'time', which are extremely hard to define with precision, have what may be called a 'grammar', in that they must be used in accordance with a set of rules. For example, 'mind' is closely related to both 'brain' and 'thought', but is equivalent to neither. In exploring concepts like these, the role of a tradition is similar to that of a language. The correct meaning of the word 'gentleman' would need some examination of the English language for its elucidation, since there is a standard given by usage. Similarly, I propose to investigate the meaning of 'providence' within a particular tradition, that of Western Christianity.[1] This is my starting point; later in the book I shall face the questions of the validity and usefulness of the concept in our own time.

This approach inevitably raises the question, 'How uniform is the Western Christian tradition?' It might be argued that there is a series of overlapping traditions, rather than a monolithic one that could give a consistent meaning to the concept of providence. However, despite the undoubted diversity that exists within what we call the Western Christian tradition, there are some relatively stable concepts within it; otherwise it would be impossible to draw some of the contrasts that we often find it helpful to make. For example, there can be said to be important differences of emphasis between the Western Christian tradition and the Eastern tradition. Moreover, these relatively persistent concepts are given additional stability by their dependence on a body of literature that has been treated as important, and often as authoritative, from the time of the Greeks. Certain works of Plato and Aristotle, and the Christian scriptures, have been a continual reference source for Western culture; and even though these works have been interpreted in many ways, they help to give the Western tradition in general a kind of core. As a result, Christianity, Judaism and Islam share, in their monotheism, many elements of a broad tradition, so that it is not meaningless to refer to the 'theistic tradition' that is common to them. The 'Christian tradition' is rather more narrow, but again refers to a core of beliefs and concepts that persist with relative stability throughout a large span of space and time.

As I have indicated, our exploration of providence is concerned primarily with the Christian tradition, although the points that I make could often be made with respect to the broader theistic tradition. Therefore my principal source for deciding how the concept of providence should be used is the Christian scriptures. However, this does not mean that the reader is being asked to accept the scriptures as revealed truth. For the purpose of this book the question of the authority of the scriptures can be put aside, or 'bracketed'; all that is necessary is an agreement that they should be taken seriously, as the embodiment and illustration of an important tradition.

I shall begin by discussing the nature of providence in a very loose way, and then proceed to a more careful analysis. My method, therefore, is rather like that of a sculptor who first makes a rough shape with a blunt instrument, and then moves on to using a fine tool.

The concept of providence is clearly related to the concept of God, but while the meanings of these concepts overlap, there are differences. Providence is concerned with changes or effects in the world, with the influence of God (some would say with his interference) in the world of nature, in man, and in history. Thus it might be said that the rain came 'providentially'; or that two people met, with far-reaching consequences for one or both of them, 'providentially'; or that a battle was won, with dramatic consequences for the history of nations, 'providentially'. Many people today would not use this language to describe significant happenings, and would disagree with the implied claims; but my point is simply that such claims are typical of an ancient attitude, and represent a traditional view of a God who is actively involved in the world.

By contrast, the concept of God, by itself, is wider. Thus the *Oxford English Dictionary*, in defining providence, speaks of the providence *of* God (my emphasis), indicating that providence is only one of the characteristics of God. God can be worshipped, or thought about, without immediate reference to his active involvement in the created order.

However, if providence refers to the active involvement of God in the created order, a puzzling ambiguity immediately presents itself. The term 'providence' is derived from the Latin *providentia*, meaning 'foreknowledge', and the related verb *provideo*, meaning 'to see to beforehand', or 'to make provision for'. The emphasis in these Latin words is not on active participation in the present, but on foreseeing, in the sense of making prior arrangements, just as I might provide for my son, after my death, by making provision in my present will. All this suggests that providence is concerned with God's ordering of things in the past, rather than with his involvement in the present, whereas popular usage seems often to be concerned precisely with this active and continuing involvement.

This ambiguity reflects one of the recurring problems concerning the nature of providence, but popular usage blurs the distinction and refers to both the foreseeing and the governing aspects of providence, though with greater emphasis on the latter. The same dual usage is found in the *Oxford English Dictionary*, where the full definition of providence runs: 'The foreknowing and beneficent care and government of God (or of nature, etc.); divine direction, control, or guidance.' We shall be concerned with both aspects of providence, but the latent ambiguity must be observed, and it will reappear in Aquinas' explicit distinction between *providentia*, in the strict sense, and *gubernatio*, governance.

We start, then, with the popular notion of a God who provides for, and is actively involved in, the workings of nature, man, and history. Providence is God in control, the 'Disposer Supreme', who 'moves in a mysterious way, his wonders to perform'. The concept continues to be used, however, by those who do not take literally the idea of a personal, interventionist God, and even by those who reject such a concept altogether. Then the concept of providence degenerates by stages into a substitute for chance, either fortunate or unfortunate. An amusing example of this emasculated usage is found in Samuel Butler, one of whose heroes exclaims, 'As luck would have it, providence was on my side.'[2] A grim example is provided by the following, written in 1904, though referring to an earlier time: 'Seafaring people look upon wrecks as their lawful prizes, gifts sent to them direct by Providence.'[3] In these and many similar examples that could be cited, there is still a suggestion that luck or chance is not pure luck or chance; there still lingers the ghost of the idea that an intelligent force is somewhere at work. However, this idea can disappear altogether. I have found one case where providence, representing a blind but somehow malevolent force, is actually contrasted with the guiding hand of God! A Norfolk landworker complains to his vicar that providence has spoilt his potatoes and turnips and has carried away his wife. He concludes, however, 'I reckon there's *One abev* as'll put a stopper on ha if 'a go too fur!'[4]

Although the foregoing examples illustrate usages of a kind, it is clear that they represent something less than the traditional concept. They are in fact illustrations of what the concept of providence is not, but can become when a secular culture gnaws away at the tradition.

If it is granted that the traditional concept of providence stands for the activity of God as he guides and governs his created order, what is it that makes the concept problematical at this time, even for many committed believers? There are three fundamental difficulties which arise out of the three distinct questions. These are:

(*a*) What kind of guidance or intervention is alleged to be involved?

(*b*) Is the claim that providence is at work in any sense an empirical claim?

(*c*) How can any intervention or involvement be attributed to the timeless and passionless God of the Christian tradition?

The rest of this chapter will be taken up with an exposition of these three questions, and the book will then continue on the following plan. The next two chapters continue to lay the groundwork for further analysis. In Chapter II, I review the historical background to the contemporary debate concerning providence, and in Chapter III I attempt to bring out the force of the typical use of the concept by a series of five analogies. The analysis is taken a step further in Chapters IV, V, and VI, which deal successively with the working of God in nature, man, and history. Because special and distinct questions concerning the nature of providence arise in each of these areas, I refer to them as the 'orders' of nature, man, and history. In Chapter VII, which is the climax of the book, I first draw the analysis to a head, and then, having explored the basic grammar of the concept of providence, I face the fundamental questions of the coherence and validity of the concept. In particular I shall be concerned with the question of whether there are reasonable grounds for employing the concept in the twentieth century. I shall argue that there are, broadly speaking, three options open to the rational mind, and that Christian belief can be a form of one of these options.

2. *What kind of guidance or intervention is alleged to be involved?*

If I am the leader and guide of a climbing party, there are at least three ways in which I can control events. First, in the initial planning of the expedition, such as the selection of suitable ropes and maps. Second, in the day-by-day leading of the party, perhaps by going first as we climb a rock face. Third, by occasional *ad hoc* decisions, made on the spur of the moment, as I deal with emergencies when they arise. This third kind of leadership may be predictable in general, in that it is certain that I shall have to deal with the unexpected, and that the kind of action that I am likely to take may be known from my character, but unpredictable in detail.

If we use this example as a crude model for divine guidance in the world, we find that it must be expanded to a sixfold model. Divine guidance or government can refer to at least six kinds of activity, although it will be obvious that these activities overlap.

I list them as they reflect increasing involvement in the created order:

   (i) The creative activity of God.
   (ii) The sustaining activity of God.
      (These two categories together correspond with the first, or planning, stage of the climbing party model.)
   (iii) God's action as final cause.
   (iv) The activity known as general providence.
      (These two categories together correspond with the second stage of the climbing party model. The emphasis is neither on prior planning nor on individual decisions, but on the smooth and predictable running of an enterprise.)
   (v) The activity known as special providence.
   (vi) The miraculous.
      (These two categories together correspond to the *ad hoc* decisions and actions made by the party leader.)

All six of these categories can refer to the activity of God, and therefore in the broadest sense all can be taken as aspects of providence. Most of the time, however, we do not find it helpful to use words in too broad a sense, and the custom has developed, for good reasons, of contrasting one kind of divine activity with another. My own suggestion is that in most contexts we restrict the use of the word 'providence' to categories four and five, and that on many occasions it is also helpful to make the further distinction between general and special providence. The reasons for this suggestion will become clear in the following sections.

   (i) *The creative activity of God.* The Christian, Jewish, and Islamic faiths stand apart from most other religions in their doctrine of a creator God, in contrast with a maker God, who used some pre-existing material, or with a God who is in some way identified with the universe taken as a whole. The origins of the creator view are obscure, but from very early times the creation stories in *Genesis* were interpreted in terms of creation *ex nihilo*, out of nothing. Unlike Plato's demiurge who, according to the account given in the *Timaeus*, fashioned the universe out of formless material, and unlike hundreds of other maker gods, the Hebrew God was held to have 'been' before (if such a temporal word can be allowed) any universe existed. God's very name, 'I am that I am',[5] was held to indicate his eternal, timeless, nature.

However, if one thinks in terms of creation, one must nevertheless allow the universe the dignity of its own order, with a relative stability and independence, once the act of creation is accomplished. It persists, and presents certain observable characteristics over a period of time. Whatever constitutes the fundamental nature of matter, whether it be sub-atomic particles, or some even more primordial element or energy form, this must have its own consistent dynamism; otherwise it could hardly be said 'to be'. The idea of pure chaos is an absurdity. This simple truth will affect our concept of providence, for it indicates that within the very notion of the created universe we already have the idea of an order that has its own laws, its own causality and its own relative independence.

Some religious thinkers have tried to avoid this implication of the idea of creation. For example, within the Christian tradition the nominalist movement in the late Middle Ages, and some Calvinists, rejected the idea of a semi-autonomous order through their desire to deny that a totally transcendent God could in any way be limited. In their 'voluntarist' views, every individual event is ascribed directly to God's absolute will, as if the universe were a grand marionette show, where every movement is solely the result of the moving finger of the manipulator. However, this view does violence to the ordinary way we think of the universe, and to the assumptions that all scientific thinking must make. It also has other serious philosophical difficulties. For example, it is quite artificial to break up all movement into a certain number of discrete events, each of which could be the result of a divine act of will, for there is rather an infinite continuum of movement. Further, divine omnipotence is in no way protected by the voluntarist theory, for who can be said to be more almighty, the God who chooses to impose limitations upon himself by creating a semi-autonomous order, or the God who cannot be limited in any way whatsoever, and therefore cannot limit himself?[6] Reflection suggests that the idea of a God who could have no kind of limitation is an absurdity which is the product of religious speculation, not the object of belief in the great religions of the world.

Since the act of creation must have produced some kind of order, it follows that in this act provision for the future is included. Whether the laws that govern change are determined and predictable in every detail from the beginning is not, however, decided by this fact, for law-like behaviour, which there must be, need not be determined in this way. The idea of creation leaves this particular matter open, though, I shall argue, other aspects of providence require that the whole future be not rigorously determined. What is laid down, or determined, in the very act of creation, is a set of possibilities, or potentialities, and in addition to this a more or less predictable pattern or picture of the universe as it can be expected to develop. Strictly speaking, the future pattern needs more than the act of creation if we think of creation merely as an originating act. We need category two (the sustaining activity of God) and perhaps categories three and four also, in order to project the future shape of the created order, but in practice it is very rare to think of creation as simply the originating act, done once and for all. People tend to include within their idea of creation either some notion of a continuing process, or elements from these other categories.

It is clear that providence in its broadest sense is involved in creation, for here the possible future is prepared, and the pattern of the kind of universe that is intended is made possible.

(ii) *The sustaining activity of God.* Closely associated with the idea of creation is that of the sustaining or preserving activity of God. For example, the Christian thanks God for his 'creation, preservation, and all the blessings of this life'. This preservation refers not only to protection from injury, but to a much more radical preservation of our very being; for without God's continual support, it is held, we should simply vanish, along with the rest of the universe.[7] From what has just been said about creation, it might well be argued that this doctrine of the sustaining power of God is redundant, since the idea of creation already includes the idea of a sustained order. Generally, however, Christians have wanted to add the doctrine, partly for emphasis, and partly to show their rejection of the deist belief that God was active in creation, but that he now leaves the universe to run itself, like an absentee landlord. The doctrine of God as sustainer certainly rules out this view.

A problem arises, however, in that the more the emphasis is put on a continuing creative activity, the more the marionette model of the voluntarist might be thought to take on flesh and blood. According to this view the explanation of a change in the universe from time t1 to t2 tends to be in terms of the present activity of God, rather than in terms of the natural consequences of the nature of the universe at time t1. In the light of this I think that it is best to think of the doctrine of the sustaining activity of God as essentially a part of the doctrine of creation, a part which emphasizes the utter dependence of all existing things on a creative act so far as their existence is concerned, such that if this activity could be conceived as being withdrawn, there would simply be nothing. It follows that the sustaining activity of God is not the explanation of change from time t1 to t2, but the upholding of an order which makes such change possible.

(iii) *God's action as final cause.* For modern man, final causality is a very obscure matter because it is part of an overall doctrine of nature, and of change within nature, that is now unfamiliar. Within this doctrine one of the essential elements in bringing about change is, in a sense that I shall try to explain, the future. In some contexts this view is easy both to state and to sympathize with. For example, if a house is being built, the finished product exerts a sort of influence on the present activity of production, because of the blueprint, and of the overall purpose of the house, when completed, as a place intended for human habitation. On Aristotle's view, all change took place in a similar way, for everything is part of a dynamic order in which things seek their natural completion. Everything was, in a sense, purposive. However, the phrase 'in a sense' is important, for the purpose displayed was not, for Aristotle, that of a creative intelligence like the Christian God. His view is better described as secular, and his purposiveness, especially that of the parts of plants and animals, had something in common with the kind of goal orientation that modern biologists ascribe to living organisms, at least in terms of species survival. But for Aristotle all change, inorganic, organic and human, took place through the operation of similar factors.

The first Christian philosophers took over the doctrine of final cause, and in their use of it two things emerge of great importance for this study. First, there developed the idea of the Christian, personal God as the final cause *par excellence*, that for the sake of which everything else is, and towards which everything moves. This is true of man in a special way, for he is seen as the crown of creation who is meant to discover fulfilment in God alone. As Augustine put it, 'O God, thou hast made us for thyself, and our hearts are restless till they rest in thee.'[8] This doctrine is crucial both for the metaphysical position implicit in Christianity, and for its devotional practice. Second, there is the notion that immanent within each part of the created order there is a dynamic movement towards its own proper function within the universe.

This latter kind of causality is often described as 'future' causality, as if what an object were destined to become somehow drew towards itself the object in the present. However, this characterization of final cause as future cause is misleading.[9] The *telos*, or

intended structure, is not thought of in Aristotelianism primarily
as a future object, but as a present force, somewhat on the analogy
of God who, as the final cause in the strict sense just alluded to,
is not there only in the future, but is also present now, and draws
all else to himself by an immanent presence.

In order to understand this point of view we must attempt to
transcend some of our own cultural categories of thought, and
try, for a moment, to forget the contemporary predisposition to
see causality either as merely a reference to observed regularity,
or as limited to the single category of efficient causation, and
entertain the idea that one of the factors that brings about change
is an in-built tendency to be a certain kind of thing. This tendency
is not a 'force' in the ordinary sense of the word, and to ask 'what'
it is, as if the answer must be some object, either present or
future, is to miss the point. The predisposition to ask this question
is itself part of the problem, and explains why it is so misleading
to translate Aristotle's four factors that account for change, the
aitia, as the four 'causes'. We have to attempt to enter into a
different overall view of nature.

However, I do not want to advocate a return to Aristotle's
categories. This, I think, would be an absurd reaction to the
realization that our own way of seeing things is not the only one.
I want simply to insist that in the traditional Christian doctrine of
nature the explanation of change was more complex than we tend
to realize.

The foregoing discussion is highly relevant to the traditional
concept of providence. If one views nature as being, as it were,
pregnant with the future, because of the operation of final causality within the very fabric of all things, then final causality is part
of the way in which the Creator, if there is a Creator, has planned
an order that develops in certain directions, without *ad hoc* acts
of the divine will. It is part of his 'provision' for the universe.
However, given the contemporary difficulty concerning the notion
of final cause, I am in favour of including this notion, together
with the notion of God's sustaining activity, as part of the meaning
of creation. But if we follow this suggestion, it must be clear that
creation cannot possibly be a doctrine of divine action only in the
past. Creation now has to stand for three different strands of
religious ideas: that of an originating act, that of the sustaining
activity of God, and that of the endowment of created things with
a dynamism that manifests itself in an activity that appears purposive. As I have stressed, this last strand is of special importance

in regard to the nature of man, for, on the Christian view, he is endowed with a nature that is restless for a fulfilment which only God himself can satisfy.

(iv) *General providence*. Not all the important writers on providence make an explicit distinction between general and special providence. Aquinas, for example, includes both ideas under his overall account of providence. The distinction, however, is useful; and when it is not made, it is often possible to detect two different emphases in a writer's thought.

General providence refers to the government of the universe through the universal laws that control or influence nature, man, and history, without the need for specific or *ad hoc* acts of divine will. Sometimes it is hard to distinguish this notion from that of creation, when that concept is thought of as a continuing activity, or from the notion of final causality; nevertheless there are differences. General providence suggests a planner who watches over and influences the general evolution of the universe, whereas the first three notions that I have discussed could be held to be compatible with a God who is unaware of, or uninterested in, the actual evolution of things. Indeed, there have been philosophies of religion that have advocated belief in such a God. However, although the notion of general providence suggests some sort of intelligent plan and oversight, this need not involve concern for individual human beings, and it does not necessarily imply what most people would regard as a 'personal' God. A personal God, as I shall attempt to show, is bound up with the notion of special providence.

A typical description of the idea of general providence is given by William Sherlock, Dean of St Paul's Cathedral in the late seventeenth century, and a well known apologist in his day. He writes: 'The ordinary government of nature does not signifie to act without it, or to over-rule its powers, but to steer and guide its motions, to serve the wise ends of his Providence in the government of mankind.'[10]

The stress here is on the general run of nature or, correspondingly, on the general movement of history. The provision of rain, for example, which enables human beings to survive, and which falls on the just and on the unjust in a fairly predictable fashion, would be an example of general providence, but the arrival of rain in the middle of a drought in response to prayer would not be. It is this kind of general providence, perhaps to be likened to a long-term pressure on natural things to conform to a certain

pattern, that lies behind religious interpretations of biological
evolution, except when these interpretations depend on special
mutations resulting from a more direct form of divine action.
Again, the argument from design is usually related to this general
pattern to be observed in nature, which, so the argument holds,
demands the work of a master planner.

In practice, however, it can be very hard to draw a sharp line
between this conception of a general providence and special providence. At the devotional level, for example, ought we to praise
God for answering our prayers when there is a 'providential' break
in the drought, or ought we to praise him for his general gift of
rain, which, for all we know, may just have happened to come at
this time? More significantly, from the point of view of this study,
this devotional question reflects a theoretical difficulty that arises
over the distinction. If general providence is concerned with the
species, as is the view of some thinkers, as opposed to individuals,
there is already the suggestion of some special act of will; for the
species is being treated differently from the rest of the biological
universe if it is in any way the object of concern as a species.

This last point can be illustrated by reference to the interesting
account of providence given by the great Jewish thinker, Maimonides, in the twelfth century. He carefully distinguishes five
theories of the nature of providence (*inaya*).[11] Among the views
that he rejects is that of the Islamic sect known as *Ash 'ariyya*,
who held that every event was directly under the hand of providence. This is the view that I shall refer to as 'universal providence', and is essentially the same as the voluntarist views I have
already mentioned. Maimonides goes on to advocate a modified
version of Aristotle, in which providence does extend below the
level of the moon, and is concerned with human individuals (contrary to Aristotle), but does not extend to individuals of other
species. Providence has no interest in flies or blades of grass, he
says, for these are entirely ordered by chance so far as individual
events go. In human affairs, however, since God always acts
justly, rewards and punishments are entirely controlled by God.[12]

So far, this would seem to be a compromise theory which would
place human beings under a kind of special providence, and the
rest of creation under general providence alone. However, Maimonides goes on to add another idea which complicates his main
theory. Providence, he says, is a kind of overflowing of the divine,
and therefore engages only the intellect. Thus only the good are
truly under providence, and only the saints and prophets com-

pletely so. 'Everyone with whom something of the overflow is united, will be reached by providence to the extent to which he is reached by the intellect.'[13]

This is a most interesting anticipation of some recent views in which God works only at the level of persons, but with the significant difference that the human level is not, for Maimonides, really made up of individuals. The influence of Aristotle is again evident here; for according to Aristotle God had no interest in human affairs, but the man of intellect, by exercising the divine part of himself, is in a sense living the life of the gods. Thus, if we interpret Maimonides in an Aristotelian way at this point, it is not really the individual who is the object of providence, for in the last resort the intellect is not individual, but part of the divine.

It is obviously hard to reconcile a view like this with Maimonides' other claim that God infallibly enacts judgment in history on all men, and it would be unwise to try. I shall suggest instead that he was an example of a thinker who was torn between general and special accounts of providence, and attempted a sort of compromise.

Despite the difficulty of drawing a sharp line of demarcation, which the thought of Maimonides illustrates, I hold that there is a difference between typical cases of what a Christian would call general providence, such as the steering of evolution towards creatures with larger and larger brains, and typical cases of what he would call special providence, such as the inspiration of a prophet with a special message for his people, or the answer to a particular prayer. The chief difficulty with the idea of general providence lies elsewhere: it is the problem of the apparent redundancy of the notion. It is one thing to state that God is at work in all natural processes, and another thing to explain what this claim amounts to. What is added by saying that God is at work, say, in the evolutionary process *taken as a whole*? Here we are very close to the issue raised in the next section, where we ask whether providence involves any kind of empirical or testable claim. If it does not, and no difference that could be observed, even in principle, arises out of the claim that providence is at work, has anything meaningful been asserted?

(v) *Special Providence.* Some scholastics divided up providence in many more ways than I am doing, for there was providence universal, general, particular, special and most special.[14] Such complication is unnecessary, but there is a significant distinction in human providence between the normal and predictable guid-

ance of an enterprise, and the unpredictable and *ad hoc* decisions
that may have to be made, as in the climbing party analogy. It
seems reasonable to make the same distinction between two kinds
of divine providence, because the biblical account of God's involvement with the world displays the same differences. God is
the author of the light and the wind and the rain, as these are
experienced every day, but he is also the one who speaks to the
prophets and chooses Saul to be king over Israel. Special providence, as the discussion of general providence has already indicated, relates to government and guidance by specific acts, even
though these acts may sometimes be of the same kind as those
that general providence provides, for example, in the case of the
rain that came in response to Elijah's prayer.[15] But the recipient
of special providence need not be an individual, in the sense of a
solitary human being, for the providential care of a group, such
as Israel, would be equally significant. As we have seen, there is
a problem latent here: how special must special providence be if
it is not to slide into the notion of general providence? However,
the root of the distinction is not the individuality of the recipient
of the providential care, but the individuality of the providential
act. Special providence is analogous to a human decision, and it
is for this reason that it is bound up with the idea of God as
personal.

A good example of the idea of special providence in the Christian tradition is given by St Augustine's *Confessions*. As Augustine
looks back on his past life, he sees the hand of God manipulating
particular events in order to forward the divine plan. The manipulation is both internal and external. He is guided away from
Manichaean ideas in part through the desire to leave Carthage
and go to Rome, a desire which Augustine sees as contrived by
providence. On the way there he is hastened by suitable winds,
a kind of external providential aid which his mother also enjoyed.[16] These illustrations are typical of the Christian tradition
from the time of the scriptures to the present day. Whether they
are to be accepted at face value or not, they are typical expressions
of belief in providence. Moreover, without a history of alleged
experiences such as these, it is hard to see how anything resem-
bling the Christian faith could have survived or spread. A concern
with individuals is an essential part of what most people think of
as providential care, for as one writer has put it; 'A deity who is
"careful of the type" and "careless of the single life" does not
exercise providence in the usual acceptation of the word.'[17]

The providential control or guidance of individuals introduces two major problems that must be faced at this juncture. The first concerns freedom. In the case of the external help which Augustine believed he had received through the winds, no special problem arises on this issue; but when he speaks of internal guidance we have entered a minefield. Augustine's own position on freedom is notoriously difficult, for he tries to combine an insistence on genuine choice with predestination. In the *Confessions* he hints at how God could guide man's choice from within without forcing it. He suggests that God directed 'by inward goads . . . that I should be ill at ease.'[18] Sherlock, in the work already referred to, has a similar suggestion when he claims that God puts a 'byas' on the wills and affections of men.[19] Since Sherlock makes an attempt to face the philosophical difficulty here, I shall describe his theory in a little more detail.

Sherlock devotes a whole section to the problem of what he calls 'moral causes', by which he means free agents, in contrast with 'natural causes'.[20] He starts with the claim that providence must have absolute control over men as well as over nature if God is to be truly God. It becomes clear, however, that he does not mean to deny all human freedom, but to insist that men's *outward* actions must be controllable in detail in order for God to carry out his purposes. His solution to the problem of freedom depends on distinguishing two kinds of divine activity within man. The first is through rewards and punishments in order to induce the actions that God wills. This is presumably the 'byas' that I have referred to, which is perhaps equivalent to the 'inward goads' described by Augustine. Evidently this produces a sort of internal pressure that *can* be resisted, and is therefore compatible with freedom; for Sherlock goes on to contrast this with a second kind of divine activity within man which has to be employed when the first does not produce the required action. (Or, more strictly, in Sherlock's philosophy, when God foresees that it would not produce the required action.) In this second kind of activity the hearts of men are turned by playing on their passions 'by an irresistible power'. Here, he says, men are not treated as free agents, but as 'instruments of Providence'. (He adds that when men are forced to do good in this way this does not make them 'good men'. It also follows that certain bad actions that are forced upon men do not contribute to their badness, and Sherlock's account of how God hardened Pharaoh's heart is along these lines.[21])

This solution is ingenious, but it will not commend itself to many Christians today, for even if it leaves a little theoretical space for human internal freedom, it undermines any adequate account of responsibility. If God is going to control absolutely our outward actions whenever it is necessary for divine justice, it is hard to see why men should be seriously concerned about the outcome of their actions in so far as they affect other people. My intentions will, of course, affect my own salvation, but few Christians are happy about a Christian ethic that is centred on what is needed for the individual's own private good. The solution that I shall recommend will involve abandoning the claim that every outward action must be under God's government, and I shall contrast this view, which is very similar to belief in universal providence,[22] with a view that allows for a radical contingency in the details of what occurs in each of the three areas that we are to examine.

The second problem reintroduces the difficulty of distinguishing general and special providence, but from a new standpoint. An analogy from what is called 'catastrophe theory' in modern mathematics will illustrate the point.[23] When the weight on a rigid structure, such as a stone bridge, is gradually increased, there may be no gradual bending of the structure, but a sudden collapse. Recent advances in mathematics have made it possible to calculate more exactly when this collapse will take place, so that what might appear as an unpredictable event can after all be fitted into a predictable pattern. Congruously, it might be suggested that many religious events that are characterized by suddenness, and have therefore been taken to be indicative of acts of divine will, may be explicable in terms of the gradual build-up of some kind of pressure, which then erupts to produce sudden changes. For example, Martin Dibelius has suggested an interpretation along these lines of the conversion of St Paul, in which the conversion becomes almost predictable if one accepts the impact of a series of other events on the conscience of Paul.[24] A convincing picture is drawn of the growing tension within a man of extraordinary devotion to what he believes to be the will of God. My point is that equivalent explanations can be given for almost every dramatic event that has been credited with religious significance. In the last analysis I do not hold that these explanations should always be accepted, but it is important to consider them as possible alternatives to the more orthodox accounts.

In order to illustrate this possibility, let us suppose that prayer for rain does sometimes prove effective. To suppose this does not necessarily mean supposing the reality of God, for prayer might sometimes be effective for naturalistic reasons, as many atheists think that it is in the case of psychosomatic cures. One factor in the build-up of rain-clouds might be the telekinetic effect of many people's thoughts. Let us suppose, further, that a number of people are praying for rain during a drought, and that this produces a sort of pressure which mingles with the other relevant factors, such as wind direction and temperature. Then on a special day a bishop makes a prayer in his cathedral for rain, and this is followed within hours by a downpour. What do we say? My point is that there are not two possible explanations, i.e., chance versus the action of special providence, but three or more. The prayer might have made a crucial difference, but not for the reason that the bishop would probably think! It could be a case of 'the last straw that broke the camel's back', in that the build-up of pressures needed just one additional element to bring the crucial change in wind. This could either be interpreted in terms of general providence, in that prayer is designed by God to exert a pressure which produces general but not absolutely predictable results, or in terms of a purely naturalistic explanation, provided that science can expand to take into account the alleged telekinetic forces.

Once again we have raised an issue that overlaps the question raised in the next section. Special providence has often been held to provide clear evidence for the presence of the divine, but reflection shows that the most dramatic events, even when well attested, do not necessarily demonstrate the activity of a God. In addition to the problem of establishing exactly what occurred, there is always the problem of interpretation. Thus the presence of special providence is never guaranteed by events; it is an interpretation of events that depends on faith. It may be compatible with reason, but it can never be absolutely demanded by it.

(vi) *The miraculous.* As we move along a line towards more obvious and invasive divine intervention in the natural order, miracles would seem to come at the end. However, even in this opening statement I have made an assertion which many Christians will disagree with. Some will not wish to make any distinction between miracle and providence, especially in the sense of special providence, and many will object strongly to the suggestion that miracles are, in any way, *interventions* in the order of nature.

I shall try to clarify this tangled issue by examining the meaning of the term 'miracle', and its relation to the concept of nature. If one looks up the English word 'miracle' in a biblical concordance it is evident that it is used to translate words standing for a wonder, or an act of power, or a sign. There is no clear contrast with the 'order' of nature, because the very idea of an 'order' of nature, suggesting a body of interlocking and autonomous laws, was not present. When the idea of an order of nature developed, in the modern sense, especially through thinkers such as Aquinas, it was inevitable that any account of miracle had to be interpreted to take note of this order. Aquinas' account of miracle is therefore of classic importance. He allows that in a broad sense a miracle is anything that goes beyond human capability and vision, but he insists that in the strict sense it is 'something that happens outside the whole realm of nature', and is therefore something that only God can do, not men, nor angels, nor devils.[25] Elsewhere a further distinction is made: the acts of creation and of justifying the sinner are not, strictly speaking miracles, because they are not effects that could in any way be produced by nature, but are in a separate and still more wonderful class. Miracle refers to events produced directly by God, which in other circumstances could conceivably have been produced by nature.[26]

Here, as all through the writings of Aquinas, we have a strong sense of the created order as having a significant autonomy. Although it ultimately depends on God as its 'first cause', it has its own 'secondary causality', which entails that it must be studied empirically for what it is.[27] Indeed, it is hard to overestimate the importance of the stand which he took here, in opposition to many of his contemporaries, both Christian and Muslim, for the foundations of what became the modern scientific movement.

In Aquinas' account of miracle there is a clear distinction between providence and miracle, when these terms are used strictly. The former involves the guidance of the created order, the latter a sort of invasion, since any scientific explanation (in the modern sense) is ruled out as impossible in principle.

There are all sorts of problems raised by this position. On the one hand, how does God interfere with or invade nature in the case of miracle; on the other, what does it mean to say that providence guides nature without interfering with it? Nevertheless, the distinction is of great importance for the mainstream Christian tradition, for providence was indeed taken to imply a divine activity that, unlike miracle, steered nature instead of overruling it. What this can mean is precisely the question that I shall be exploring in Chapters IV to VI, which deal with providence in nature, man, and history.

Accounts of miracle by liberal theologians in this century have almost all taken a different tack. They have defined miracle in terms of what causes wonder, and above all, in terms of what has religious significance for men of faith.[28] That these are vital elements in the analysis of the miraculous is certain, but whether they are sufficient to define the nature of miracle is still, in my view, questionable. If these are the only defining characteristics of miracle, then miracles are to be singled out from other events by considerations that are ultimately psychological, for what has religious significance is not necessarily dependent on some objective feature of the event. Although it is possible to use the word 'miracle' in this way, I question whether such a usage captures the sense of the word as it has been used by most Christians. Ordinary usage does imply some contrast with the natural order, once the idea of a natural order is established. (This last point indicates that this is an issue that cannot be resolved simply from biblical usage.)

To illustrate, consider the miracle of the Feeding of the Five Thousand.[29] There have been various naturalistic explanations to cover what is described: for example, the 'miracle' may have been the extraordinary charity evoked, which made everyone share the lunch that he had hidden away for himself. However, if this were the true account of what happened, most Christians now, and just about all in former ages, would be inclined to say that, although what happened was marvellous, it was not truly one of the biblical miracles. The miracle, for most believers, was tied up with an astonishing and *unaccountable* multiplication of loaves and fishes. The main reason why some Christians want to remove this element of unaccountability from their definition of miracle is that they do not believe that such strictly unaccountable things ever happened. Therefore, if they are going to continue to speak of miracles, they have to redefine them in a way that makes them possible and believable. But perhaps clarity would be served better by saying that they no longer believed in miracles, as that term has usually been understood.

However, there is an important complication. Even if we allow talk of an 'order' of nature, it is misleading to think of this as a totally enclosed set of laws or principles. The concept of nature is constantly changing and expanding as science advances. I have already suggested, for example, that factors such as telekinesis, which are abhorred by many but not all scieɪ tists, may one day be included, like hypnotism,[30] within the bounds of respectable science. This consideration is especially important when we consider the famous healing miracles of Jesus, or of later times, for we are beginning to imagine explanations of a sort for many of these within terms of psycho-somatic medicine, and it would be odd to suggest that this proved that Jesus' healing miracles, except for the raising of the dead, were not really 'miracles'.

Furthermore, I tend to agree with the claim that there is something misleading in defining 'miracle', as Hume did,[31] in terms of events that are violations of, or contrary to, nature. Even if one thinks in very Thomistic language, the order of grace does not go *against* nature, but completes it, or adds to it, in a way that is somehow congruous with its whole purpose. Similarly, Aquinas' claim is that no naturalistic explanation of a miracle could ever be complete, rather than that a violation of nature has taken place. Likewise, C. S. Lewis, after attacking the view that miracles are contrary to the laws of nature, defines them in terms of events that are peculiar in not being 'interlocked backwards' with the rest of nature.[32] However, it follows from this view too that no natural explanation could ever be complete.

It is evident from this discussion that it is extremely hard to find a satisfactory definition of miracle in the context of the modern world. Before I attempt to resolve the problem, two further points must be made.

First, the attempt to clarify a concept does not always stop at analysis; very often there must also be a recommendation as to what usage will be more helpful in the future. In a useful account of the nature of clarification, D. D. Raphael has summarized the procedure under three items. First there is analysis, where the elements are specified. My breakdown of providence, in its broad sense, into six categories, is an example of this. Second, there is what he calls 'synthesis', where the logical relationships of concepts are worked out. The discussion of the relationships of providence to miracle is one of many examples of this during this study. Third, there is the improvement of concepts for the sake of clarity and coherence. My recommendations concerning the relationship of providence to the autonomy of nature, man, and history will constitute my most important attempt at improvement.[33]

If we accept this account of clarification, it follows that the present discussion is not concerned simply with discovering the 'correct' meaning of miracle, for there is confusion and disagreement about its use. One has both to examine how the word has been used, and to suggest the most profitable usage for the future, a usage which must, however, be closely related to former practice, unless we are going to coin a new word.

Second, the mention of the impossibility of a full explanation of miracle is ambiguous. Both special providence and miracle, when the latter is defined in Aquinas' sense of an event that goes beyond nature, cannot be *fully* explained by wholly naturalistic means, but for different reasons. An act that is said to fall under special providence, if minutely examined by a scientist, would not demand some extra-causal factor from his point of view. When nature is 'steered' by providence, there is not held to be any physical mystery. However, the man of faith would insist that the full explanation of the event must include the way in which God guided man, or nature, and what he purposed in this guidance. But when a miracle, in the sense under discussion, is said to be not fully explicable by naturalistic means, a much stronger claim is being made. There is the suggestion that the scientist would be unable to give an adequate causal explanation from his own point of view, for example, in terms of the physics and chemistry of the event.

I shall now attempt a resolution of this problem, and my quandary in doing so can be illustrated by referring to two miracles *par excellence*, the resurrection and the incarnation.

An examination of what Christians have traditionally believed about the resurrection tends to support the view that a miracle must not have a fully naturalistic explanation. If Jesus really died, in the sense of suffering physical brain decay of a kind that has always so far resulted in the permanent loss of the brain, and if he were nevertheless seen by a number of witnesses to have a physical body, or a quasi-physical body, that was alive three days later, then clarity would not be served by insisting that there could be an explanation of this in terms of a richer understanding of the possibilities latent in the natural order. Of course, many recent interpretations of the resurrection avoid this full-blooded account of the alleged event, and speak in terms of psychic experiences, or intense feelings of the presence of Jesus, etc. It is not my purpose to discuss which account is right, but to point out that, if these radical interpretations are accepted, there is an important sense in which, as with the example of the reinterpretation of the Feeding of the Five Thousand, something that was believed is no longer believed. Many Christians would claim that, even if some of the significance of the event can still be maintained, there was no longer a miracle, in the proper sense of the word. For the traditionalist there certainly was some kind of invasion into the natural order from the order of grace.

The counter-argument consists in claiming that it is precisely the significance for man that constitutes the presence of miracle, and a 'spiritual' interpretation of the resurrection might preserve the essential significance of the event. Moreover, an examination of the incarnation can be held to support this view. To start with, in so far as the incarnation is linked with the doctrine of the virgin birth, many Christians do not believe that the virgin birth, in its literal as opposed to its symbolic sense, is important. For them the incarnation, therefore, need not be associated with an inexplicable event at the time of the birth of Jesus.

But in a way this last point is only of incidental importance, for the incarnation must not be confused with the doctrine of the virgin birth: it is, rather, a metaphysical doctrine about the true nature of Jesus. It is hard to see how any physical event of a kind that necessarily defied scientific explanation could be essential to the 'miracle' of the incarnation when viewed in this way. Even a verified virgin birth would not verify this claim. This seems to support the view that a miracle does not owe its essential status to its inexplicability, but to its significance.

However, we are not yet clear of the difficulties, for the incarnation is not a typical case of a miracle in the Christian tradition. The logic of Aquinas' position should lead him to place it, along with creation and redemption, in a quite special category, because none of these are events within nature. Usually, when we speak of a miracle, there is an event in public history, and a source of wonder in the event itself. But the physical event of the birth of Jesus was very ordinary, discounting problems concerning his conception, and in fact this is part of its significance, paradoxically, for the Christian. What is special about the event is necessarily not public, for there could not be sensory evidence concerning Jesus' relationship to the divine, since the divine is spirit and not body. However, a typical miracle has involved an event, or alleged event, like the raising of Lazarus,[34] where the amazing nature of the event has been public.[35]

All this suggests that it may be a mistake to look for a definition of miracle in terms of the old-fashioned concept of definition, whereby there is a single, common characteristic which links all cases together. As is the case with many difficult words, 'miracles' may be linked together instead by a kind of family resemblance, as a result of which there may be clear criteria for applying the word 'miracle', but no one absolute criterion. However, I do propose to argue that the impossibility of a fully naturalistic interpretation is a typical and most important characteristic of miracle. In taking this conservative stand I am influenced by two particular factors. One is the awareness of how much Christians in the past have used claims about miracles as evidence for their faith. Even though I believe that they were wrong to use miracles in this way, and were at variance with the practice of Jesus,[36] this factor indicates clearly a part of what Christians meant by miracle. The second is that I happen to hold a view of the resurrection which many readers will regard as very old-fashioned, for I do take seriously the possibility that a unique physical transformation of the body took place, a transformation that defies all naturalistic explanations. Since, for reasons that I have explained, we are both examining how the word 'miracle' has been used, and recommending how it should be used, it is not improper for a personal factor such as this to influence my proposals. By the same tokens, it is very natural that some Christians want to use the term with the emphasis being placed much more on the religions significance of an event, and, like John Macquarrie, banish the notion of 'supernatural intervention' from the concept.[37] Thus, while the usage that I recommend is more typical of the classical Christian tradition, I do not want to deny the possibility of an alternative approach. This alternative would mean accepting that there is no essential difference between what I have called special providence and miracle: there would only be a difference of emphasis, since 'miracle' tends to refer to the more spectacular and the specially significant. However, I shall adopt the practice of contrasting special providence with miracle, along the lines that Aquinas uses to contrast providence in general with miracle, since I find it helpful to indicate in part what providence means by indicating what it is not. In its strict sense, providence is the guiding or steering of nature, man, and history; it is not the manipulation of these orders by the introduction of causal factors which would lead a scientist to be mystified.

I have now completed my initial examination of the six elements that can be considered to make up what providence can stand for when that term is taken in its broadest sense. From now on I shall be concentrating on elements four and five, that is, the elements known as general and special providence, and shall contrast these concepts with others, including those of creation and miracle.

3. Is the claim that providence is at work in any sense an empirical claim?

Most Christians have held that providence is to be trusted not only on sheer faith, but on evidential grounds. The grounds put forward have been the same as those put forward to support belief in God, only with the emphasis on God as governor rather than on God as creator. However, in recent years the attitude to the claim that there is evidence for providence has been much changed, for the alleged evidence is suspect not only to agnostics and atheists, but to many Christians as well. At one extreme we have some Christians who still maintain the traditional Roman Catholic view that many of the essential truths of religion can be rationally demonstrated; at the other extreme, we find followers of Karl Barth who deny any validity to natural theology, and who believe in some form of providence purely on faith. Between these extremes are others who hold that there are grounds for belief in providence, but that these have to be expressed in a way that is different from that of most former defences of faith.

Two principal grounds for faith have been urged, one centring on the argument from design, the other on personal experience. The argument from design starts with the recognition of the universe as a structured whole that provides the necessary context for human life. The beauty of the universe is emphasized, and above all the complex series of inter-related factors which together make it a suitable environment. The argument is ancient, and has received especially influential expression in the writings of Paley.[38] Even Kant, who rejected all the arguments for the existence of God except for his own version of the moral argument, regarded it with great respect.[39] However, the scientific movement in general and the theories of Darwin in particular, have virtually destroyed the argument as an argument. (It may have some other role, for example, that of evoking wonder.) Many thoughtful people still believe both in evolution and in the creative work of God, but there is a crucial difference between believing that evolution is *compatible* with a religious explanation of life, and believing that it *demands* it. Few people would doubt their theoretical compatibility, but equally, few believe that a religious explanation is demanded when the extraordinary suitability of the environment for human life can be explained in terms of successive adaptations. It is not a case of the environment happening to suit the animal: the environment has determined what kind of animal can flourish.

The position is more complex than this brief discussion suggests, and, as we shall see in Chapter IV, there are still many Christians, including some eminent scientists, who believe that the argument from design can be restated in order to retain some force. However, it is clear that the argument cannot give empirical grounds for belief in providence in the straightforward way that was once believed. In particular, if an 'empirical argument' is taken to be the kind of argument that is used in physics, one which should be accepted by all rational minds once the evidence is presented, then the argument from design is not such an argument.

The other principal ground has been personal experience. I have already given examples from Augustine's *Confessions* of the kind of personal testimony that is referred to, and countless other cases can be cited. For example, there are stories of people running orphanages who find themselves continually facing economic ruin, and who, after prayer, time and again receive 'providential' help.[40]

Unfortunately the evaluation of this kind of claim is notoriously difficult. Apart from the obvious difficulty of establishing the outward facts, there is the constant problem of their interpretation. In some ways the situation is similar to the problem of evaluating the evidence for the paranormal, for in both cases people tend to jump for the interpretation that they are looking for, often being unaware of other possibilities. In attempting to evaluate this kind of experiential evidence for providence I shall put the sceptical case first, and then see if an adequate counterargument can be provided on behalf of those who claim that there is experiential evidence for providence.

In many Italian churches and shrines one can see monuments in which God, or the Virgin, or some other saint, is thanked for a preservation from storm or disease. A sceptic, on seeing these, is said to have remarked, 'Where are the monuments of those who perished?' The remark can be made into a general point, for the enthusiast for any occult phenomena tends to disregard negative instances. A related weakness in his reasoning is often the broadness of his generalizations, which makes it hard to *identify* negative instances. This is notoriously the case in most astrological predictions. With providence the situation is the same, for we note the timely rain, and forget the hundred ordinary rainfalls, and the dry days when we longed for rain. Also, we may say that we 'find' God in a beautiful day, but 'finding' God is such a loosely analysed set of feelings, and refers to so broad a generalization, that it is hard to identify negative instances, i.e. of when God could not be found.

Some observations concerning probability support the sceptic's case. In a way 'the improbable is probable', as Cicero pointed out long ago.[41] For example, if we dig up one hundred prehistoric skulls, ten may have holes in them, and one a fairly round hole. If we dig up a million, at least one will have a surprisingly round hole. Yet I have heard the argument put forward that the discovery of just such a round hole proved that the animal had been shot by an extra-terrestrial visitor many thousands of years ago! Of course, the odds are a million to one against the next skull having a really round hole in it, but if we look for long enough we shall find such a skull.

This illustrates the point that all people are going to have some experiences that are astonishing, and a few people can be predicted to be going to have experiences which are even more astonishing, and so on. Inevitably some of these experiences will look as if they had been designed, and it will be almost impossible to persuade those who have them that they are the 'one in a million' for whom such experiences can be expected.

Along such lines it is easy to see how the sceptical case can be pursued, but let us now try to see the case for the other side.

First, what a religious man who believes in providence is concerned with is not any odd coincidence, but events which seem to have special significance. Logically, it must always be possible that such events are the result of chance factors, but if the sceptic insists that the explanation *must* be in terms of such factors, then his position is question-begging and just as faulty as that of the person who used the round hole to prove that flying saucers had landed. The possibility of there being some special factor at work, some agency of a radically different kind, cannot be ruled out *a priori*, unless the statement 'all events have purely naturalistic explanations' is merely a tautology. Thus, even if proof for the presence of a special factor is not possible, a person who has what seems to him a number of significant experiences, a number that goes beyond what he considers he might be expected to have by chance, is quite entitled to entertain the hypothesis that some radically different factor is at work. Moreover, he will not entertain this hypothesis in isolation from the knowledge of other people's experiences, and it is in the light of these that sometimes even a single experience may cause him to reconsider his whole interpretation of life.

The suggestion that a 'radically different factor' may be at work must be stated very carefully. What is being posited is not a causal factor of a kind that a minute physical examination of the event could show to be required. The analysis of the concept of providence already undertaken shows that providence in its strict sense is not manifested by this kind of causal gap. The suggestion that a 'radically different factor' is at work refers to an existential claim about the meaning of life, and a metaphysical claim about the nature of reality, not a scientific claim about what a repeatable experiment or observation might bring to light. These experiences, it is argued, point to an explanation that has to be superimposed upon the scientific explanation. However, the grounds for this are not simply feelings; there is what the religious person would regard as evidence of an appropriate kind, in that the interpretation leads to expectations about life which future experiences may bear out. There is, therefore, some analogy to the procedure of scientific testing.

The suggestion that a providential interpretation may properly be entertained as a result of personal experiences is certainly controversial, but all that I am claiming at this stage of the argument is that it is wrong to rule out the possibility of such an interpretation *a priori*. Such a rejection of the suggested providential interpretation is based on the view that factors not amenable to scientific investigation cannot be real, and this view can easily be dogmatic and question-begging.

Up to a point the situation here is like a wholesale rejection of psychical research. For example, in *ESP. A scientific evaluation*,[42] C. E. M. Hansel has argued that all cases of the apparently paranormal should be put down to either chance or fraud. Several reviewers have argued[43] that Hansel brings an *a priori* assumption to bear throughout his analysis, and that this tends to rule out the possibility that extra-sensory perception is real because of its potential embarrassment to certain scientific procedures. The result is a search for naturalistic interpretations with the underlying assumption that these *must* be there if only we look carefully enough. There is, however, an important difference between the evidence for ESP and for providence, for many of the ESP phenomena, if genuine, are, or should be, susceptible to strict scientific testing. An essential part of the argument, therefore, is whether or not certain results have been demonstrated to have taken place. On the other hand, the alleged 'evidence' for providence is not open to this kind of testing, and it is this fact which raises the special problems that I am now discussing. Both believers in providence and sceptics face great intellectual dangers at this point. The danger for the believer lies in using the absence of strictly scientific criteria as a *carte blanche* to follow his wishful thinking, and to believe what he likes on scanty or inappropriate evidence; the danger for the sceptic lies in misunderstanding the nature of the claim that is being made, and also in failing to consider the possibility of an alternative way of looking at reality because of his prejudices. There is nothing in the methodology of science that compels the scientist to believe that only what scientific method can examine is real.

The suggestion that I have been leading up to is that we should distinguish between (1) a scientific hypothesis, which is to be tested by public procedures well known to science, and (2) a personal hypothesis, which by its very nature is open only to private testing, or testing by a group, but which may nevertheless be a matter of judgment rather than of caprice.

Behind this distinction lies a claim that there are some facts and interpretations which all should accept when the evidence is produced, and others which it is rational for one person to accept while others remain agnostic or sceptical. Examples of the former are usually found where an experiment or observation can be repeated in the presence of others, but repeatability is not an absolute precondition, since there may be massive public evidence for an historical fact. With regard to the latter, my first example is of a non-religious kind. At a criminal trial I am giving evidence that runs counter to everything else that is reported. Let us say that I was the only one who witnessed a respectable citizen kill his wife, and that while this deed was done there was a criminal lunatic in the room. Let us further suppose that it turns out that I stand to gain financially if the respectable citizen is found guilty, and that there is other circumstantial evidence to link the murder with the lunatic. In such extreme circumstances it would be rational for all people, except myself, to believe one thing, but for myself to believe another, and in this case I should in fact be right.

In such bizarre cases a rational man would doubt the evidence of his own senses; 'Was I perhaps hallucinating?', he would ask.

But it is not essential for my point that the witness can *know* a truth which only he should believe, only that he may be rationally entitled to believe something where other people are not.
Let me move on to a case that is both less extreme and more relevant. A certain Christian is in the habit of praying for sick people in his district, and he notices that some of the people he has prayed for are healed. He then begins a systematic watch for the effects of his prayers and is astonished by the apparent connection between his prayers and cures, so that a personal hypothesis that his prayers are effective becomes verified in his judgment. This judgment cannot be verified adequately by others, since only he knows whom he was praying for silently, when he was concentrating most, etc. If he informs others of his plans, they may to some extent share in his tests, but never from the standpoint available to him. This would be a case, it might be argued, where, even if the Christian were in fact mistaken because what had actually happened was a one-in-a-million run of coincidences, he would be rationally entitled to believe in the connection while others might not be.

However, there are two major objections to this suggestion which must be considered. The first is likely to come from a broad range of Christians and other theists who will ask: 'Is this the kind of evidence that Christians actually find themselves confronted with?' Although few Christians would deny that the sick are sometimes helped by prayer, many are highly dubious about claims concerning the regular or systematic efficacy of prayer with regard to physical health, since they run counter to their understanding of God's presence in the world. Some of the more radical Christians, such as Bonhoeffer, find themselves stressing the *weakness* of God in the world, a weakness that must be deliberately undertaken if man is to be made truly responsible, a weakness dramatically emphasized in Jesus's humble birth and ignominious death.[44] Because of this they do not expect prayers to be answered by dramatic cures, but look instead for evidence of a much more elusive kind, namely in the experience of a grace that enables them to live with their problems, and to do something themselves about other people's problems, rather than in an experience of these problems being taken away. Thus, while I have much sympathy with the idea of 'an experimental faith' as canvassed by Alister Hardy,[45] and find his suggestion similar to that of the 'personal hypothesis', I do not think that most people who make such suggestions are sufficiently aware of the problem of the nature of the evidence, and of the problem of its evaluation.

This objection can be given depth by pointing to an interesting stream in biblical piety which supports the view that God should be worshipped regardless of worldly benefits. This is a strand of thought which, if taken seriously, must profoundly modify one's understanding of providence in the order of nature. The best example is in the prophet Habakkuk:[46]

> Though the fig tree do not blossom, nor fruit be on the vines, the produce of the olive fail and the fields yield no food, the flock be cut off from the fold and there be no herd in the stalls, yet I will rejoice in the Lord, I will joy in the God of my salvation.

Passages such as this must be treated with caution, for some writers in this vein were looking for benefits for Israel in the long run; but there is no doubt that in the later prophets there was developing a sense of the intrinsic duty to worship God, and of a relationship based on love rather than on contract. It must also be remembered that the Old Testament writers did not believe in a personal after-life, except as a kind of shade, and this strengthens the claim that some of them were suggesting that God is to be worshipped simply for what he is. Not only is this far removed from the egotistical religion of John Locke, and of many others,[47] but there is the implication that faith is not dependent on personal experiences of providence in the world of nature. Some recent religious movements have taken this emphasis to its limit and totally removed any belief in divine providence from the Christian faith. I am referring to some of the non-cognitive views of religious statements, such as those of R. B. Braithwaite.[48] These views are interesting, but are clearly outside the mainstream Christian tradition with which I am concerned.

The second objection will come from the sceptic. Suppose that we allow that an individual may have a set of experiences which makes it rational for him to suspect that some special factor is operative which cannot be observed, why should he entertain the possibility that this additional factor could be what some people call 'spiritual'? Why not fraud, or some as yet unknown force that may have a naturalistic explanation? Why introduce the totally new and unnecessary category of providence, with all the problems that relate to the meaning of that concept?

However, the insistence that the introduction of a spiritual interpretation of some experience is to bring in a new and un-necessary category is the expression of a conclusion, not the state-ment of an established fact. The proper analysis of our whole experience, prior to any suggestion of verifying a particular per-sonal hypothesis, is an extremely difficult and controversial mat-ter. While some accounts of perception stress the prime role of the senses, others see perception as a much more complex pheno-menon in which the data supplied by the senses have to be unified by a series of factors supplied by the mind. These factors, it may be argued, enshrine all our experience in a rich context in which there is not only awareness of objects, but also of values and of persons.

The claim that experience is value-laden is familiar, and while still controversial, it has gained credibility as many philosophers have become increasingly disenchanted with strictly empirical accounts of our experience. One important source of this disen-chantment is the work of Chomsky in linguistics, and the growing evidence that all human language is, in part, the result of a genetic endowment. Language therefore *grows*, rather than is learned by observation. As a result, we inevitably interpret the world through the categories supplied by our language.

The claim that experience has a personal or spiritual component is similar to the claim that it is value-laden in that the suggestion is made that, alongside our awareness of physical bodies through our five senses, we become aware of *persons*, as centres of a self-consciousness that is like our own. If this is true of our ex-perience in general, then mention of the 'spiritual' is not necess-arily the importation into language of a redundant 'extra'; it is rather the unveiling of an element already present in our overall perception.

None of these observations proves the legitimacy of religious language, but they certainly call in question the assumption that it is *illegitimate* because it is not factual, in the ordinary sense of that term. It follows that when someone suggests a providential interpretation of some experience, and entertains what I have described as a 'personal hypothesis' that providence is at work, we must beware of dogmatic, *a priori* rejections of the very nature of the hypothesis, just as much as we must beware of wishful thinking and of the drawing of unwarranted conclusions.

We are now in a position to summarize an answer to the ques-tion 'Is the claim that providence is at work in any sense an empirical claim?' A number of responses can be made.

First, the general answer must be yes. The point is not that religious people are necessarily justified in their claims concerning providence, but that for most of them some kind of what they regard as evidence is an important basis for their faith. The word 'empirical' is perhaps misleading, and it is probably better to refer to the claim as 'experiential'; but it is necessary to emphasize that 'sheer faith' is not the only, and not the most common, basis for a religious person's beliefs. Moreover, the kind of evidence that is considered appropriate is not so vague that religious people cannot say on occasions, 'That is not good evidence for this doctrine, but this is.' In other words, they do not simply accept people's feelings, they frequently argue about the weight of various bits of alleged evidence. Thus certain experiences are treated as evidence. Whether they are good evidence is a separate question.

Second, different religious people have somewhat different expectations about where to look for evidence. Until recent times nearly all would have looked for dramatic series of significant coincidences, like those recorded by Augustine, or the experience of the orphanage director, etc. This seems to have been the kind of expectation that the first Christians lived with. Other Christians look for evidence of a much more elusive kind, that is, for spiritual effects within their own personal struggles to live out the Christian life. They will test, for example, the claim that 'God is faithful, and he will not let you be tempted beyond your strength.'[49]

Third, the situation with regard to general providence is different from that regarding special providence, and this may help to clarify further the distinction between them. For belief in general providence, 'evidence' is relevant only in the sense that everything, taken as a whole, is said to point to the need of such a factor. This is certainly not a straightforward sense of the word 'evidence', and relates to general metaphysical arguments that ask questions about the 'whole'. On the other hand, belief in special providence is tied up with what religious people regard as evidence, not in the sense of *all* that happens, but in the much more normal sense of *this* experience, in contrast with others. It is in this sense of 'evidence' that providence is related to an experiential claim within the Christian tradition.

One interesting complication in the problem of evaluating personal experience must be mentioned here. We noted that a person would not be likely to assess his own experience in isolation from what he knows of the experience of others. In practice this is of great importance and helps to explain the influence of the Christian or other scriptures. In so far as one man's personal experience tends to correlate with that of others, the situation ceases to be simply a matter of a personal hypothesis; for the very fact, if it is a fact, that certain kinds of experience are general, makes some claims about human nature more plausible. There is still the problem of the proper interpretation of these experiences, but the suggestion that they can be accounted for in terms of the one-in-a-million chance, or of some personal idiosyncrasy, becomes less plausible in so far as research exposes a common core in the religious experience of different people.

Before we pass to the next section, one further point of great importance must be made. In principle, reflection on the nature of God or of providence can be undertaken in two ways. There is first an approach 'from below', as men try to understand and interpret their experience of particular things, or their experience of the whole order of the universe as it appears to them. Second, there is an approach 'from above', through an attempt to work out the truth about God and his activity from first principles, seeking the inherent logic of God himself. The former approach roughly corresponds to the old idea of natural theology, and reflects a method that can loosely be called *a posteriori*. (It is not strictly *a posteriori*, since the experience reflected upon is not only sensory experience but also religious experience, such as that of the numinous. Nor is this first approach strictly that of natural theology, since some of the experiences reflected upon may be regarded as revealed.) The latter approach is essentially *a priori*, and is exemplified in the thought of Plotinus, Proclus, and others who seek to work out what providence is from the essential nature of God.

In the context of this distinction it is clear that the emphasis throughout this study falls under the former approach. Hence from my point of view the claim that providence is at work is, in a broad sense, an empirical claim, or better, an experiential claim. However, the importance of the latter approach must be noted, both for its historical importance and for its intrinsic interest. There are still those who seek to explore the concept of providence from within their understanding of the very nature of God and of his creative activity, and while this is not my method, I respect the endeavour, and remain agnostic about its possibilities. For those involved in such a search, providence will not be an experiential concept, except perhaps secondarily.

4. How can any intervention or involvement be attributed to the timeless and passionless God of the Christian tradition?

Crudely put, the last two sections have asked 'What is providence?' and 'How do we know that there is a providence?' The issue faced in this section is less often considered, because it seems more remote and abstract than the other two, but in the last analysis it is the most fundamental of the three questions. The God of the Christian tradition is required by both logic and devotion to be transcendent, the 'wholly other', who is eternally beyond and behind the temporal order. At the same time he is alleged to be immanent within it. Problems concerning transcendence and immanence are raised for all theists, but for Christians, with their doctrines of a Holy Spirit and an incarnate Son, the issues are especially acute.

The idea that God is changeless and eternal, in the sense of transcending the category of time rather than simply being everlasting, is rooted in certain Old Testament passages, and more particularly in certain Greek ideas of the One. In patristic teaching it reaches its complete form. Thus Augustine, using a graphic illustration, imagines God as an infinite and eternal sea in which the whole created order is immersed like a sponge. The sponge is both utterly surrounded and utterly penetrated by this sea. Moreover, the sea is measureless.[50] Later, Aquinas advocates a similar doctrine with his claim that God enjoys an eternal present,[51] and an eternity that is 'an instantaneousness whole lacking successiveness'.[52] God cannot therefore *fore*know, for this would put him into time; rather, he simply 'knows'.[53] Also, like Augustine, he analyses the love of God in terms which deny any kind of appetite or passion.[54]

The logical ground for this teaching is the doctrine of creation. If God is the source of the created order that exists in space and time, yet he himself is neither part of it, nor all of it, then he must transcend the orders of space and time, however hard it may be to conceive of such a transcendence. If time began with creation, as Augustine forcibly argued,[55] then God is not old, but timeless. If creation is surrounded and penetrated by God, as in Augustine's analogy, then God is not huge, but spaceless. The devotional ground for this teaching is the concern that God must be worthy of worship, and therefore, in Anselm's phrase, 'that than which a greater cannot be conceived'.[56] Behind this concern lies the ancient view that perfection implies changelessness, for the eternal

and perfect order of heaven is contrasted with the flux and un-
certainties of the lower world.

For Plato and Aristotle, the problem of relating a personal and
perfect God to the world did not arise in the same way, for their
ultimate principles were not active in the way that the God of the
theists is. Ultimately they were the cause of all change, but anything corresponding to special providence was either denied or
left to subordinate 'gods'. In the Old Testament the problem is
implicit but little discussed. That some writers were sensitive to
the issues is, however, evidenced by the increasing concern in
later Judaism with mediators with an ill-defined status, especially
the concepts of Wisdom, Word, and Spirit.[57]

When the question is asked, 'How can one combine the view
that God is transcendent with the view that he is immanent?',
there are, I suggest, three possible kinds of reply. The orthodox
'solution', if it is such, is a strange blend of all three.

First, one can stress the paradoxical nature of the joint belief,
underlining the claim that there must be a mystery here that goes
beyond human understanding. This claim can take several forms,
but the only one that I can begin to consider seriously is the one
that does not speak of an ultimate unintelligibility or contradiction, but that stresses the inherent limitations of the human mind.
In this version of the claim, God is intelligible to himself, and
increasingly so to those who begin to enter his light, but is systematically incomprehensible to those living on a lower plane. Analogies often used here are those of a dog's understanding of his
master's thoughts, or our use of paradoxical models in science
which expose different aspects of a truth which we cannot consistently combine in a literal sense. The most familiar example is
the treating of light as both a wave and a stream of particles, with
the implication that its reality is neither. In such paradoxes there
is no glory in irrationality; we just accept the *apparently* irrational
when experience seems to force us to such a view. In contrast,
some religious writers appear to have gloried in irrationality for
its own sake.

Second, one can attempt to explain, at least to a certain degree,
by the use of analogies. The very attempt to do this has a certain
assumption built into it, one that takes up the suggestion in the
last paragraph concerning those who begin to enter the divine
light. Despite the gulf between God and man, perhaps something
of the divine light is present in all human reasoning, so that our
gropings after understanding are not *totally* blind, otherwise the

analogies would have no point. However, there is a systematic tendency for this approach to collapse into the first approach, for whenever one sees the limitations of an analogy, or realizes that it has been pushed too far, one tends to refer to the impossibility of a full understanding. Job speaks for all religious writers when he exclaims, 'I have uttered that I understand not'.[58]

Third, taking up a theme in the Old Testament, there is the approach to God through a mediator. In one form or another one finds this approach in all the world's religions as they try to deal with the absolute, especially when they descend to a popular level. 'Filling in the gaps' seems to be a response of both logic and of the emotional drive. Plato has his demiurge and a galaxy of Forms below the Idea of the Good; Aristotle has an array of unmoved movers; most forms of Buddhism have their Bodhisattvas, and so on. The most extreme versions of the attempt to fill the void with a host of descending intermediaries is found in some of the Gnostic sects, such as the system of Basilides.

At the level of piety, this approach to the absolute through someone or something lower seems very understandable. It is often pointed out that prayers through the Virgin, or a favourite saint, or a 'sacred heart', have a similar motivation. However, at the level of logic, despite a superficial attraction, there is a fatal flaw in this approach. So long as God is conceived as a gigantic version of a human hero, there is everything to be said for approaching him cautiously, by a succession of steps; but if God is infinite and eternal, as in the Christian tradition, then no such steps can bring one any nearer. To use a mathematical illustration, the gap between number two and infinity is the same as the gap between number one and infinity. There is a sense in which one might be moving in the right direction, but, somewhat paradoxically, one never gets any closer. This is a good illustration of the problem of man's approach to God, for here too there can be a strong sense of moving in the right direction, plus an awareness of an everlastingly infinite gulf. One man can be meaningfully better than another, but neither is beginning to be like God in substance. Christians do speak of 'unity' with God, but except in certain heretical variations of Christianity that have been influenced by monism, this has not referred to a substantial unity, but a unity of relationship.

Given this logical difficulty, how can the idea of a mediator help to bridge the gulf? Christianity has attempted a startling and original answer to this question, in which, precisely because the gulf is infinite, it has somehow to be overcome by God himself, and the mediator is therefore both God and man. Incarnations of a kind are common in the world's religions, but not this claim that a monotheistic absolute is uniquely related to a single human form in a once-for-all act of identification.

We shall return to this theme in Chapter V, but the obvious difficulty is quite simply, how can Jesus be both human and divine? At this point, approach number three, like approach number two, tends to collapse into approach number one, that of paradox and mystery. There can be no human explanation, but, so the argument goes, experience compels us to assert both the humanity and the divinity of Jesus.

Christianity, as we see here, has produced a blend of these three approaches, a blend which is unimpressive to the sceptic. However, I think that a certain defence of the emphasis on mystery within this blend is in order. It has been argued by many scientists that the universe is not only stranger than we imagine, but stranger than we can imagine, and this brings out well the fact that whatever the ultimate truths may be concerning the nature of the universe, some of these truths must transcend our powers of reasoning. If the universe is infinite in space and time or both, then as a whole it presents similar baffling qualities to the concept of God. If the universe turns out to be finite in any sense, then equally baffling questions arise concerning its limits in both space and time. Thus the man who attempts to speculate about the universe as a whole cannot be expected to produce the kind of straightforward theory that would be appropriate to a more limited subject. What we ask of him is rather that he try to root his speculations in human experience and observation, and that he try to be as consistent as possible. By the same tokens, theological speculation cannot be judged by the canons of chemistry, but it does not follow that one argument is as good as another.

It must be clear from all this that the third issue that I have raised concerning the concept of providence, although the most fundamental, is the one where I shall make least claims for the success of my analysis. However, I shall regard the little I say as successful if it makes the reader more aware of this underlying difficulty of any talk of providence in any monotheistic religion.

One further point must be made in this introduction. Within the Christian tradition some recent thinkers have brought forward the radically new idea that God himself may not be altogether changeless, but may be evolving, along with the universe. In

Whitehead, the most important of these thinkers, there is an eternal aspect to God, in that his purpose and character are changeless, but his knowledge of events changes as these events unfold, and therefore there is change of a kind within God. With Whitehead and his followers we have moved outside the mainstream tradition on which I am concentrating; however, some further references will be called for in later chapters. This is because Whitehead's views are taken so seriously by many Christians that his ideas underlie important growing points in the tradition. Although there is a relative stability in the tradition, as I have indicated, it is not static, and the doctrine that God is unable to suffer in himself is under reconsideration by many thinkers who in other ways regard themselves as orthodox Christians. Moreover, this is one of the areas where there is a gap between orthodoxy and the understanding of Christianity by the ordinary Christian, who may well think of God suffering with him, and of being concerned with him, in ways that cannot comfortably be accommodated to the orthodox doctrine of the passionless God of Christianity.

An equally important aspect of Whitehead's thought concerns the view that in order to safeguard both God's freedom and the freedom of the created order, God has to work characteristically by persuasion rather than by coercion.[59] One consequence of this philosophy is that the classical account of what it means to say that God is omnipotent is called in question. As the analysis proceeds it will appear that I have considerable sympathy with Whitehead's approach to this issue.

II

The Historical Background

A large book could easily be written on the different ways in which God or the gods have been thought to be active in the world, or indifferent to it. In this chapter I shall describe only certain views that have been crucial either for the formation or for the development of providence as it is found in the Christian tradition.

1. The Old Testament

No single word in the Old Testament corresponds to the English word 'providence' until we come to the late apocryphal book called the Wisdom of Solomon, written in Greek, probably around 100 BC. Here the Greek *pronoia*, forethought, is used twice to refer to God's oversight.[1] However, the ideas of divine provision and government are implicit all through the Old Testament, and the absence of any special word for providence is probably due to the fact that it would never have occurred to the Jewish writers to contrast events in which God was active with those in which he was not. God was responsible for all that happened, even though some events, like the crossing of the Red Sea, were held up as marvels of a special kind. Every event, good or bad, was willed by God. As Amos put the matter, 'Does evil befall a city unless the Lord has done it?'[2]

For later men, such a view raised acute problems concerning human freedom and God's responsibility for sin. It led, for example, to the well-known scholastic distinction between God's *permissive* will, in accordance with which absolutely everything happens, and his *active* will, which does not force itself on nature,

39

for nature is allowed to follow its own laws except when miracles
occur, nor does it force itself on man when he is acting voluntarily.
However, the biblical writers, like their Greek contemporaries,
did not feel that there was a problem of freedom arising out of
their belief in divine government. E. R. Dodds, in a classic study
of Greek religious ideas, has described how ancient people would
often have several complementary accounts of why certain events
happened. Such events are what he calls 'overdetermined'.[3] Similarly, there are plenty of indications that the Hebrew writers held
men to be responsible for their actions, and to have a power of
choice,[4] and that they witnessed a growing sense of individual
responsibility that began to replace earlier notions of collective
guilt.[5] All these things were affirmed at the same time as the
apparent counter-example of a man being likened to clay in a
potter's hand.[6] One can impose a sort of consistency here by
claiming that God directed only outward actions, while men were
free in their inmost thoughts, along the lines suggested by Sherlock; but it is better simply to admit that from our point of view
events were 'overdetermined', for there is little doubt that the
biblical writers tended to think that God could control human
thoughts.

Within the Old Testament it is possible to detect at least four
of the six aspects of providence discussed in the introduction.
There is creation,[7] though creation *ex nihilo*, strictly speaking, is
an interpretation of *Genesis* rather than its explicit statement.
There is the sustaining activity of God, and his general government of all things, equivalent to general providence, though these
two themes are run together in several biblical passages, such as
in the great nature poem, Psalm 104.[8] In addition, there are
dramatic happenings which would later be described either as
examples of special providence or as miracles. Although the
writers would not themselves have made this last distinction, for
reasons that I have already discussed, they do provide different
kinds of account of wonderful events which lend themselves to
this distinction when it is made. In the case of the crossing of the
Red Sea both kinds of explanation are given for the same event.
Thus we hear that 'the Lord drove the sea back by a strong east
wind,'[9] but in the next chapter, and probably from another ancient
source, we hear that 'the floods stood up in a heap'.[10] In other
words, sometimes the marvel concerns the religious significance
of an event that a natural explanation could be given for, and
sometimes the marvel could not possibly have a natural explana-

tion, and indeed this very impossibility is part of the point. Perhaps the clearest examples of the last type of event are the signs given to Gideon.[11]

In summary: the Old Testament gives continual testimony to belief in an intensely active and personal God, one who both provides for and governs the world. However, the writers were not much given to speculation, except for some agonizing over the problem of evil. The implications of their belief in providence were left to a later age to work out.

2. The New Testament

Turning to the New Testament, we find that the Greek *pronoia* is not used, except once when it refers to human forethought.[12] But, as in the Old Testament, the concept is everywhere implicit. For example, something akin to general providence is implied when the Father is referred to as the one who 'makes his sun rise on the evil and on the good, and sends rain on the just and on the unjust'.[13] Another relevant passage, and one that seems to straddle the notions of general and of special providence, goes: 'Are not two sparrows sold for a penny? And not one of them will fall to the ground without your Father's will.'[14] This is a difficult verse to interpret, since it may mean that the Father causes the fall, or it may mean simply that he is aware of it; but the verses that follow make it clear that God is at least concerned with the lot of every human individual.

When it comes to special acts of God that could later be classed as examples either of special providence or of miracle, there is an interesting contrast between the synoptic gospels and John. In the synoptic gospels there are many accounts of the miraculous, but their symbolic significance is not stressed, except as a general sign of the nature of Jesus. For example, the disciples of John the Baptist are asked to tell him what they have heard and seen.[15] In general the miracles are wrought on account of compassion for the sick and hungry, and we find frequent admonitions by Jesus not to publish the marvels abroad.[16] In the Gospel of John, on the other hand, the individual miracles are seen as symbolic in themselves, and not only as indicative collectively of the nature of Jesus. Accordingly, when the author of John refers to a miracle as a 'sign', *semeion*, he is thinking of the significance of the particular event, such as the turning of water into wine.[17]

Strictly speaking, this mention of miracles may seem to be

relevant only to the concept of providence in its broader sense, but miracles are also important for the notion of special providence in the New Testament because of their connection with the belief that God is personal. At the root of the claim that God is personal is the view that he is concerned with individuals. The word 'concerned' must be interpreted with care, for, as we have seen, in the orthodox account no passion is said to be involved, but at the least a watchful awareness plus a perpetual offer of grace is included. For the Christian, the principal ground for belief in a personal God is the love or concern for individuals shown in the character of Jesus, who is held to mirror in time the character of God in eternity. In the life of Jesus a concern with individuals is certainly evidenced by many things, such as the time and trouble spent with people of no social importance, and with women and children; and it is clearly expressed in parables like those of the lost sheep,[18] and in the use of the Aramaic, *Abba*, for 'Father'.[19] The miracles of compassion are part of this general picture.

Over all, therefore, the New Testament presents a portrait of an intensely personal and active God, which is the foundation for the Christian doctrine of special providence. If one wishes to indicate actual examples of special providence in the New Testament, I would suggest that for the Christian the actual words and actions of Jesus are the most important examples. Apart from the allegedly miraculous episodes, these are manifestly 'natural', in the sense that they illustrate the use of nature rather than its suspension, but on a Christian interpretation they are all particular manifestations of the love of God himself.

3. The Greek background

In his *The Greeks and the Irrational*, E. R. Dodds has warned us against over-emphasizing the rationalistic elements in Greek religion, for in the religion of the average Greek there were far more elements of the irrational, or what is perhaps better called the 'non-rational'. Nevertheless, I am going to concentrate on certain key themes in the rationalistic religious thought of Plato and Aristotle because of their extraordinary influence on the Christian tradition.

In the scale of reality, or 'the great chain of being', the ultimate principle for Plato is the One, a subject which he treated with reverent caution, and probably lectured on once a year to his inner diciples.[20] This 'One' is perhaps to be identified with the 'king of all' in Plato's letter,[21] and almost certainly with the Idea of the Good, familiar to readers of Plato's *Republic*. In the account of the Good we immediately recognize many of the characteristics of the Christian God. It is eternal, changeless, and one, in contrast with the temporary, ever-changing, and multiple order of the physical world. Though impersonal, and unaware of the individual, unlike the Christian God, it is the focus of contemplation and of a kind of worship. Moreover, although not directly involved in the lower world, it is of crucial importance for it. For example, when Plato likens the Good in the eternal world to the physical sun in the natural world, he stresses that the sun is not only the brightest object, it is also the means by which we see all objects.[22] Here there is at least an echo of the idea of divine grace, for the Good is not only just there, it illuminates us and draws us towards itself. This theme is further worked out in the allegory of the cave,[23] and in the *Symposium*. In the latter the various speeches in honour of *eros*, although in some cases expounding views that Plato would not have endorsed, build up a sense of the role of *eros* in binding the universe together, and acting as a kind of driving force to maintain the movement of each part. This is especially evident in the contribution of the physician, Eryximachus.[24] At the climax of the work Socrates' speech then describes the levels at which *eros* can drive man.[25] At the level of sexual attraction *eros* quite properly dwells on the beauty of the human body, but unfortunately the majority of people stop here, and fail to see where *eros*, as the hungry desire and search for what can truly satisfy us, is really meant to lead us. But those with discernment pass on from the contemplation of physical beauty to the beauty of the soul, like the mature lover who cares more for the character of his beloved than for his appearance. But this too is only a beginning, for we are to be led on to the beauty exhibited in the abstract forms and in the sciences, until the few will come to see Beauty in itself, in a mystical experience wherein the Idea of Beauty is found to be identical with the Idea of the Good.

Although much impressed by the poetry of this passage, most modern readers cannot take Plato's convictions about reality seriously, and their reasons for this are similar to those underlying their rejection of the Christian idea of God. In particular, modern man is taught to divorce the science of the 'true' from the 'ought' of the moral order and from the appeal of the beautiful. In Plato, such division is monstrous, for the ultimate explanation of all movement is the One, which can of all things most truly be said 'to be', and to which we *ought* to respond as *eros* draws us to its beauty. For Plato the ultimate reality is, at the same time, the Good, the True, and the Beautiful.

Aristotle's God has many similarities to Plato's One. There is not the same emphasis on God as the object of our contemplation, but in some other ways, in so far as he differs from the Platonic doctrine, he comes closer to the Christian conception. As G. E. R. Lloyd has pointed out; 'His conception of God is certainly not an entirely impersonal one. He is alive, and his activity, contemplation, is described as supremely pleasant.'[26] The more rational a man is, the more he imitates this activity of contemplation, and thereby he can up to a point share in the divine activity,[27] even though, as with Plato, there can be no question of God being aware of man, no point in any kind of petitionary prayer, and no possibility of friendship with God.[28] God is totally absorbed in the contemplation of his own nature, hence the strange-sounding description of God as 'self-thinking thought'.[29]

Nevertheless, this remote God is the source of all movement, and his existence and fundamental nature can be demonstrated, since they are demanded in order to explain the world that we experience. This view must be explained in the context of the famous doctrine of the four causes. Aristotle held that any adequate account of movement had to locate four distinct factors, *aitia*. Only then have we properly dealt with the 'why' of anything.[30] His own illustration of the building of a house, which has already been alluded to, is helpful here.[31] The material cause is the matter out of which the house is built, the formal cause is the plan or blue-print which the builders copy, the efficient cause is the energy exerted by the men at work or the machines they use, the final cause is the purpose for which the whole enterprise is undertaken. Without all four of these factors there would be no movement, and no house. In theory, therefore, it should always be possible to distinguish the four factors in any movement, but in practice this is often hard, and in the *Meteorology* Aristotle makes the illuminating comment that 'the final cause is least obvious where matter predominates', and in fact he makes no mention of final cause in his explanations of meteorology.[32]

In theory not only are there always four factors at work, but the final cause is properly the highest explanatory factor.[33] With this in mind we can build up Aristotle's model of the universe. Basic to this model is what was later to be known as the Ptolemaic astronomical system, in which a series of concentric spheres revolved round the earth. The physical order comprised the whole sublunary system, and consisted of four essential elements, earth, water, air and fire. This was the world of flux and change. Surrounding this were the celestial spheres, made of a fifth element, ether, and here the motion was eternal and changeless. These celestial spheres, especially that of the sun, which is nearest to the moon, act upon the sublunary order, imparting movement as efficient causes, though exactly how the contact between the celestial spheres and the physical sphere is made is not satisfactorily explained.[34]

The critical question now arises, 'How is the motion of the celestial spheres to be accounted for?' Not, according to Aristotle, by an infinite series of the same kind of sphere, for then we would simply be multiplying entities without in any way explaining the whole system. Thus the search for an explanation of movement demanded an unmoved mover who was not part of the series, but was, we might say, of a totally different category of existence. Each sphere in the series receives its source of motion from the next sphere and in a sense interacts with it, but the unmoved mover, if it is to bring an end to the chain of causes, must be both unmoved by any sphere beyond itself, and in no way be affected by the sphere which it draws. Therefore, the unmoved mover, Aristotle's God, must act solely as final cause, drawing the nearest celestial sphere, not by acting as an efficient cause, for this would 'drag down' the unmoved mover, and destroy its transcending nature, but as the object of love, *eros*.[35]

This account is much complicated by Aristotle's insistence that there must be a series of unmoved movers in order to account for the complex movement of the planets so that strictly speaking God is the *first* unmoved mover, but this does not affect the essential model. God's existence is necessary for the explanation of movement as a whole, and hence we arrive at the argument from motion that has become one of the standard 'proofs' of God's existence.[36] Also important is the tremendous influence of this picture of God as necessarily changeless if he is to be truly God. The divine mind does not change, 'for any change would be for the worse and would imply some kind of process'.[37] Rightly or wrongly, this aspect of Aristotle's God, an aspect that echoes the nature of Plato's One, was accepted by the Christian philosophers, and this leads to the third issue discussed in the introduction. Thus, for Aristotle, the question of God's providential action in the world did not arise, for his providence did not extend below the sublunary sphere, and even above it the mechanism of providence was entirely through the attraction of *eros*. The lower spheres would not have moved at all without God, and in this sense one could speak of the influence of God, akin to a very remote general providence, but anything corresponding to special providence, or even general providence when this refers to regular pressures on the natural order, could be only through the agency of lower beings.

Arising out of Aristotle's theology is a general issue that it is convenient to take up at this juncture, that is, the place of metaphysical arguments in support of any doctrine of providence. Aristotle's argument that there must be an unmoved mover is a typical example of reasoning about the explanation of the *whole* of reality, and such arguments have played an important role in the history of Christian speculation. However, as Hume pointed out,[38] we cannot assume that questions about the whole universe have answers like questions about parts of the universe, for by definition we cannot have other universes to compare with this one. Whether or not it is proper to ask questions such as 'Why does anything exist?', or Aristotle's 'What is the explanation of movement as a whole?' is a controversial issue, but whatever our response may be to the issue of their status as questions it is certain that they are not empirical questions.

This may appear to be contradicted by my use of the argument from design when discussing whether providence could have empirical support. However, one of the interesting things about this argument when it is used by Paley and his followers in order to demonstrate providence is the fact that they draw it away from its character as a metaphysical argument, and turn it into an (unsuccessful) scientific argument. They tried to cite particular evidences for design. Now that alternative, Darwinian explanations can either be demonstrated or reasonably conjectured, the tendency is for the argument to change back to its earlier form as a metaphysical argument, e.g. about the implications of the evolutionary process as a whole. Thus the argument enjoyed a period when it seemed to take on new life as a scientific or quasi-scientific argument, and it is under this guise that I considered it as a possible basis for an empirical claim concerning providence.

4. The Christian synthesis

As is widely recognized, Christian thought in the first few centuries was a complex mixture of Hebrew monotheism and Greek philosophy. This is viewed very differently, by some as a disaster, because alien categories are alleged to have been imposed on the purer Jewish roots, by others as a providential happening, because a richer and more fruitful philosophy emerged than could otherwise have been the case. In any event Christopher Butler is right when he writes, 'If the Church was to convert the Graeco-Roman world, it had, sooner or later, to respond to the challenge of Greek philosophy. For this challenge, though Greek in its provenance, was really the challenge of the human intellect itself.'[39]

The philosophical nature of Greek thought and the unphilosophical nature of Jewish thought can both be exaggerated, but nevertheless there did emerge a new blend of two very different traditions, Greek and Hebrew, with four dominant elements in the formation of the concept of God: the God of Moses and the prophets, the Father of Jesus, the Good of Plato, and the Unmoved Mover of Aristotle. One could add to these four basic sources, for example, by including Philo's *logos*, or the Stoic 'Reason', in order to show that it was not simply a case of two ideas mixing, but of two complex, and occasionally parallel, streams joining to form a common river. It is in this context that one must understand the development of the Christian concept of providence, and of the related ideas of incarnation, trinity and redemption. In the Christian synthesis there is the attempt to combine (1) an ultimate source of the whole universe that is perfect, changeless, and eternal, with (2) a personal God who watches over and guides events in nature, man, and history, exercising forethought and government.

Since this book is not primarily an historical essay, I shall concentrate on the statement of the Christian position, in Aquinas, one of the great systematizers of the church. The key to Aquinas' position on the relationship of God to the world lies in his distinction between primary and secondary causality. The context for this distinction was Aquinas' reaction to the Islamic Neo-Platonic philosophy of his time, a philosophy that by its power and comprehensiveness was threatening to capture the mind of educated Europe. As Charles Martel stopped the might of Arab armies near Poitiers in AD 732, so, argues Gilson,[40] Aquinas stopped the advance of an Arab philosophy which would have been equally devastating for Christian culture in the thirteenth century. This apparently 'academic' matter, in the negative sense of that term, was in fact of the utmost consequence for world history. What was at stake was a conflict between a view in which all things, including God and man, were utterly determined, and Aquinas' view that there was a radical freedom both within God himself, and within the order that he had chosen to make. It was a consequence of this latter position that the natural order could intelligibly be studied for its own sake, and hence the foundations for an empirical science could be laid, as we have already noted.

The Arab philosophy was backed up by all the weight and authority of Aristotle, a factor that it is hard for us to appreciate, living as we do in an age that is rightly suspicious of 'authorities' in questions of truth. For some centuries the Arab philosophers had had the corpus of Aristotle available to them, and the depth and comprehensiveness of his system gave any philosophy apparently based upon it a great authority. Aquinas was one of the first Christian philosophers to be able to make use of this corpus, and he interpreted it very differently at certain crucial points. According to Aquinas, God, as first or primary cause of all that is made, has chosen, in a free act of will, to create a physical order that can make itself. In doing so it exercises 'secondary causality', and demonstrates a genuine autonomy, an autonomy seen especially in the crown of creation, man. Strictly speaking, this is only a relative autonomy, for God has created the cosmos, sustains it, and governs it both by providence and by the occasional miracle, but the explanation of why things happen in nature is consistently to be sought in the regular powers of nature. He therefore attacked the idea that the explanation should be in terms of necessity or of God's direct action. 'If effects are not produced by the action of created things but only by the action of God . . . we are deprived of all knowledge of natural sciences, in which, preeminently, demonstrations are made through effects.'[41] In support of this claim there are frequent references to God's use of intermediaries, or second causes. To deny their power is in fact to detract from the creative power of God,[42] for this amounts to making the order of nature pointless.[43]

This emphasis on the autonomy of nature is coupled with an emphasis on the need for a first cause in order to explain the existence of the whole natural order. Here the dependence on Aristotle is very evident. God is seen as final cause, and 'the final cause is the cause of all the other causes',[44] for without it there

would simply be nothing, just as the purpose of house-building
calls into operation the other three factors. Furthermore, all order
in nature points to this final cause. 'Things which do not know
the end do not tend towards the end unless they are directed by
one who does know, as the arrow is directed by the archer. . . .
This is the work of providence.[45] Aquinas is here going beyond
Aristotle's insistence on the necessity of a final cause in order to
account for nature, because Aquinas' final cause has to know and
will what is happening. In addition, God is operative, according
to Aquinas, not only as final cause, but also, in a certain manner,
as formal and efficient cause as well.[46]

Aquinas' specific teaching on providence must be understood
within this more general account of nature, a nature that must not
be reduced to a set of *a priori* principles overflowing from the
'One' in necessary stages, but as an order with its own inherent
causality and dignity. It is a fallacy, he reiterated, to believe that
we can magnify God by belittling nature.

When he turns to deal with providence directly, he considers it
in relation to prudence. In man, prudence is the virtue that leads
us to foresee and provide for the future, both for ourselves and
for those subject to us. By analogy, we can describe the nature of
God's prudence or providence, but given his changelessness and
completeness, his providence relates only to those subject to
him.[47] This providence has two aspects: under the first, which
refers to the strict meaning of the term, God plans for the natural
order, and here, Aquinas claims, God provides for all things
directly. Under the second aspect God exercises government, and
here he normally works through intermediaries.[48]

On reviewing Aquinas' overall position the most obvious question that the modern reader will raise brings us back to one of the
principal themes of this study. The question concerns the mechanism of providential action, and this becomes especially pertinent
when we recall Aquinas' sharp contrast between miracle, in which
God acts apart from secondary causes,[49] and providence, where
he does not act apart from them, but rather 'interiorily in all
things'.[50] Can there be a middle ground between out-and-out
autonomy on the one hand, and miracle, in the traditional sense
of a divine intervention in the natural order, on the other? I shall
try to face this question in the next section, and then again in
Chapter III.

By and large Aquinas' position with regard to providence has
been that of Christianity in general since his time. There have

been some, both Catholic and Protestant, who have espoused a universal providence, but these have never been a majority. Calvin, for example, held that God's government directly controlled every event, for, as he put it, 'not a drop of rain falls without the express command of God'.[51] Superficially this view, which has had considerable influence in Presbyterianism, resembles the Arab view which Aquinas rejected, but the overall positions are different. Calvin wanted to give complete freedom to God, and none to the natural order, although he tried to argue that man was still somehow responsible, and 'free' in a significant sense. The Arabs, against whom Aquinas was writing, had wanted to give no freedom to God or to the natural order, while Aquinas had wanted to give a limited, but appropriate, freedom to both. God could not act contrary to his nature, but he was free to create in an infinite number of ways: man is limited, but he must have the kind of freedom that makes him responsible, and able to respond to grace. This last position, as I have indicated, is the most typical of Christianity. Hooker, for example, restated the essentials of Aquinas' position for Anglicanism, especially in his account of the system of laws that govern both God and man.[52] The distinction between general and special providence is not made by Aquinas, but it can easily be made from within his position, as it was by many of his followers. John Wesley also makes this distinction, though with a slightly different emphasis. He distinguishes the providence which 'presides over the whole universe', and watches over organic nature and animals, from the 'superintending providence which regards the children of men', and this latter he then divides into three degrees of particular providence.[53]

5. *Modern science and the Christian reaction to it*

Even in nominally Christian countries, the intellectual climate has changed dramatically since the hey-day of Christian philosophy. This has come about gradually, and often without any explicit rejection of the old terminology, so that the vastness of the change is often obscured. Modern man still speaks of providence, but as we have seen, except for a minority this does not indicate belief in the active participation of God in the world. By far the biggest reason for this change is the impact of scientific thought from the sixteenth century onwards. In the early days nearly all the scientists were men of strong religious convictions, despite the troubles that they ran into with the established churches, but they were introducing a revolution in the way in which people thought about the world, a revolution that was bound to undermine traditional philosophy. Also, at one particular point many of them did challenge the very terminology of the former Christian philosophy, namely in the matter of final cause.

The manner of the rejection of final cause has to be stated carefully, for it was not as blunt as is often supposed. Francis Bacon, who was one of the major advocates for its elimination from science, wrote: 'The inquisition of final causes is barren, and like a virgin consecrated to God produces nothing.'[54] This is much quoted, but it must be remembered that Bacon was not in fact against the search for final causes in metaphysics, or in sciences that have to do with human action.[55] Also, although Bacon was very influential as a writer, he was not in the forefront of actual experimental work. Harvey, who was, is happy to speak of the final cause of the heart, namely 'the circulation of the blood'.[56] However, this too must be assessed with care, for in the context it is clear that Harvey was thinking of what some would later call an 'intrinsic final cause', along the lines of a kind of functional teleology that many biologists imply when they relate parts of living organisms to their wholes. This provides no ground, by itself, for belief in an 'extrinsic final cause' of a kind that was a basis for the teleology of Aristotle or Aquinas. Harvey did not deny that there was this extrinsic final cause, but it was irrelevant to his thoroughly empirical method.

Thus some reject the language of final cause, including Bacon, Descartes,[57] and Hobbes,[58] some continue to use it; but what is happening is that a new way of looking at the universe is emerging. This new way has historical roots in Aquinas' account of the relative autonomy of the natural order. However, not only is this autonomy taken much more seriously, but also the manner of its working is seen under a radically different model. This is nowhere clearer than in Newton, the devout theist, who, in Barbour's words, saw the world as 'a structure of forces and masses rather than a hierarchy of purposes'.[59] Instead of being something akin to an organism, the world order is like that of a clock, to be explained in terms of the properties of its smallest parts (a view that Whitehead has strongly opposed[60]).

Within this context of the vast clock, providence takes on a new character for those actually aware of the scientific spirit of the age. God's work is primarily to be seen in the way in which the great machine is set up, and Descartes and others often speak of

God as 'first cause' in a way that sounds like an echo of Aquinas, but is in fact very far from his meaning. For the clockmaker the emphasis is on 'first' in a strictly temporal sense. This position leads naturally to deism, which, in its extreme form, holds that God is unconcerned with the running of the machine. Oddly enough, however, few thinkers actively espoused deism, and certainly not most of the leaders of scientific thought. They tended to accept the possibility of miracle, and, like Newton, to speak of God having to make occasional adjustments to the system. But although they might thereby preserve some kind of Christian faith, it is hard to see how a significant belief in providence could survive, except for the many who were not really aware of the implications of scientific method, or for those who were able to indulge in some kind of 'double think'.

This is a good moment to pick up the problem of the mechanism of providential action that we passed by after summarizing Aquinas' position. In a sense Aquinas has no answer to the question, 'What is the mechanism of divine action?', but he might well have objected to the way in which the question is put. To ask for the 'mechanism' is to ask within the context of the clockwork model, and this very model may systematically rule out any answer that would retain something corresponding to what Aquinas meant by providence. Within Aquinas' model, in which there is a hierarchy of ends, it would be misleading to suggest that there was a problem concerning how a higher purpose can be effective, for the model itself allows many kinds of factor that together form the explanation of change.

If the clockwork model of the universe had persisted as the dominant one for all men of science, then there would have been the following options open. (1) One could simply oppose the scientific spirit of the times and stick to an alternative way of looking at the world, rather in the way that many fringe sects of Christianity now oppose some of the findings and assumptions of contemporary science. (2) One could abandon the concept of providence. (3) One could modify it, in order to take away the idea of God moulding nature to his own ends without violating its autonomy, for example, by restricting the scope of providence to the spiritual experiences of man. All three of these reactions can be found, but the eventuality that calls for them all to be seen in a new light is that the clockwork model has not persisted as the dominant scientific model. The situation in contemporary science is much more complicated than many people realize, and the idea that something corresponding to a traditional account of providence must be ruled out by any acceptance of the scientific spirit is premature. Contemporary science tends to be far more cautious than the science of the nineteenth century, and less dogmatic about our ability to understand the workings of the universe.

So far I have been concerned in this section to show how the scientific enterprise has raised problems for the concept of providence because it has appeared to rely on models that leave no room for it. At a more popular level the issue has not been, 'Can belief in providence be squared with the acceptance of scientific method?', but the gradual build-up of the feeling that providence is redundant, whether or not it is formally in contradiction with scientific assumptions. Although there may be no necessity for the scientific spirit to destroy the religious spirit, there is in practice a powerful tendency for the former to *replace* the latter. The religious explanation of why things are as they are, even if not a rival to a scientific explanation, tends to be less and less referred to, and eventually ceases to be significant. Meanwhile most people come to forget what the concept of providence actually signified.

There is an illuminating analogy here in the gradual secularization of political thought during the same period. For example, Lilburne, the seventeenth-century Leveller, began writing tracts on man's religious citizenship, attacking popery, but increasingly he became concerned with man's secular citizenship, and he saw his radical views here as a consequence of his religious position.[61] A little later, Locke attacks political theory that is solely based on the exegesis of the Bible, and bases his philosophy of the state on 'reason'.[62] By the nineteenth century, the switch is complete in many writers, and in Marx we find a political theory that is avowedly materialistic. Here is a parallel with the secularization of science. Newton, Lilburne's younger contemporary, produces a secular physics that is allegedly rooted in Christianity, and Laplace, at the end of the process, argues that God is an unnecessary hypothesis. In both cases religious accounts give way to compromise accounts in which there are both religious and secular interpretations, but where the two accounts are not essentially related, and then these accounts in turn give way to purely secular accounts. The analogy is all the stronger when we recall that the high water-mark of the process, in both cases, was the nineteenth century. Now, both in science and in political thought, there has been a reaction, not back to the religious explanations of the past, but away from the extremes of Laplace's mechanism and Marx's materialism.

Thus the secular, scientific movement produced a two-pronged attack on the concept of providence. At the popular level the concept appeared increasingly redundant, and removed from the concepts actually being used in scientific, political, and other areas, including morals, law, and art. At a more academic level, but ultimately responsible for this feeling of redundancy, was the actual undermining of religious concepts by the adoption of modern ones that sometimes formally contradicted them, and sometimes left them otiose.

Even in the early days of modern science, some Christian apologists were aware of the long-term implications of the scientific movement, and attempted to produce a Christian philosophy adequate to the challenge. One such was Ralph Cudworth, the Cambridge Platonist, who deserves more attention than he gets. In 1678 he published his theory of 'plastic nature' which he saw as an alternative, on the one hand to the view that God governed everything directly, and on the other to the view that everything happened by chance.[63] Throughout his work Cudworth is extremely anxious to do justice to the traditional Christian faith, with a strong Thomistic emphasis on freedom, and equally anxious to do justice to modern science, for example in his approval of Harvey's work, and his defence of the atomic theory. However his arguments are, in the main, disappointingly unoriginal. He relies on the many 'particular phenomena in nature, as do plainly transcend the powers of mechanism',[64] a type of 'God of the gaps' argument which is inadequate for reasons to be explored in Chapter IV, and also on the metaphysical claim that the whole system of regularities could not be based on chance. This is essentially a restatement of Aquinas' argument.

Nevertheless, Cudworth is important, because in his account of plastic nature he is attempting to find a compromise between the two models of the universe, that of the hierarchy of purposes and that of the mechanical clock, and he makes a bold effort to characterize his plastic nature through a series of analogies. Using ideas drawn from Aristotle's account of nature, he likens the operation of plastic nature to human art, only with the difference that plastic nature works immediately on matter, as a kind of 'inward principle', as if a heap of stones had an inbuilt tendency to form itself into a building.[65] This activity is very similar to the notion of general providence, only there is less emphasis on an intelligent plan, and more on a quasi-force inherent in nature. It might be described as a concept that lies somewhere between that of final cause and of general providence. He claims that plastic nature 'doth drudgingly execute that part of his providence, which consists in the regular and orderly motion of matter', and he contrasts this with what he calls a 'higher providence' which corrects and occasionally overrules the workings of plastic nature.[66] This latter is needed because plastic nature cannot act with election or discretion, while election is the hallmark of the 'higher providence'. This is very close to my identification of special providence with particular acts of divine will, other than the miraculous.

Cudworth's book is interesting and suggestive, but it certainly did not succeed in slowing the drift towards a secular outlook. In part this was occasioned by the excessively pedantic apparatus which Cudworth used, but the principal reason was the sheer momentum of the move towards a radically different view of nature. No apologist succeeded in halting this drift; all that could be done was to keep alive an alternative way of looking at the world.

The total result of the scientific movement and of reactions to it forms a very complex picture so far as the contemporary understanding of providence is concerned. This understanding is affected by the inadequacy of many people's view of contemporary science, and also by the significant and rapid changes that have been taking place within science, and again by many people's inadequate grasp of the traditional concept of providence itself. In this situation any attempt to state a Christian philosophy, or to criticize it, must include some clarification of the concept of providence. Such clarification must make use of helpful analogies, and to these I now turn.

III

Analogies for Divine Action

1. The use of analogies

In the first chapter we began to explore the difficulties to be faced in giving an adequate account of providence, but despite these difficulties it became evident that the Christian tradition demanded such a concept if it were not to slide into materialism on the one hand, or some kind of nominalism in which God directed all things miraculously on the other. Christianity has attempted to find a middle ground between these extremes, and therefore it urgently needs adequate analogies in order to express its point of view.

This need for adequate analogies was given further weight by the second chapter. The historical background to the concept of providence explains the crisis that the intelligent Christian (and in a rather similar way, the intelligent Jew or Muslim) faces in the twentieth century. The thought-forms of science, which affect our whole culture and influence the world views of non-scientists as well as of scientists, seriously call in question the traditional Christian philosophy of providence. This does not prove that what was held in the past was false, but it does show that if there is any truth contained in the Christian tradition, it has to be restated for our time. This is required, in particular, because our new insights into the law-like character of the physical universe, and of man, and of history, appear to make a doctrine of providence redundant.

The use of analogies in the philosophy of religion needs no apology, for we use analogies in many areas of thought, including science. Indeed, we use them whenever we have to stretch words in order to do justice to the reality we seek to express. But we must note the limitations of arguments from analogy. They are not proofs, nor even evidence, for the reality of the relationship that is described. They can have suggestive force, but their basic function is one of illumination or explanation.

The most common form of analogy used in religious language has four terms, although the analogy may not be expressed in a way that makes this clear. It is not simply a case of 'A is like B', but the more complex case of 'As A is to B, so C is to D'. In the Psalms, for example, we read 'Like as a father pitieth his own children: even so is the Lord merciful unto them that fear him'.[1] Here it is claimed that we can liken God's fatherhood to human fatherhood. We might say that we stretch the word 'father', or use it analogically, to refer to God, but strictly the claim is that there is an analogy between two relationships, one that we know well, the other that we are beginning to discern.

In the case of religious analogies like the above there is a special problem that must be noted. In non-religious uses the normal situation is that we are thoroughly familiar with one usage of a word, which is its principal or proper use, technically called the 'prime analogue'. The word is then stretched to apply to derivative analogues. Aquinas' classic example will serve to illustrate the point.[2] 'Healthy' is a word that refers primarily to the condition of an animal, but it can be applied analogically to a medicine that is conducive to health, to food that preserves health, and to (the correct) urine that can be a sign of health. The special problem with religious language is that in most cases the prime analogue is not the term with which we are familiar, as in the above example, but God. Thus God's fatherhood, of which we know little, is the proper or full fatherhood, and is therefore the prime analogue, whereas human fatherhood, of which we know much, is the derivative. In other words, the religious analogy is the opposite way round to that which we find in normal situations.[3] We dimly discern something of God's fatherhood from the best human parents, from the mother just as much as from the father, and then, if we are able to learn more of the true nature of fatherhood, we have to apply this back to the human situation, and learn what kind of parents we should be.

This must suffice for the basic nature of analogy in religion, but the last point will reappear as of great importance when we return to the question of the 'personal' nature of God.

In the next five sections I am going to explore five suggested

analogies for the relationship of God to the universe. The first
two are ancient; the next two are original so far as I am aware,
though I would not be surprised to find that someone had used
similar analogies; the fifth again is basically ancient.

It should be clear from what I have said about the nature of
analogies that when I present an analogy, and then discuss its
merits and limitations, I am seeking to illuminate something that
we already dimly grasp, like Paul's present knowledge which he
likens to puzzling reflections in a mirror.[4] I want to be quite
explicit here about an assumption that I am making, an assumption discussed in the introduction. Those brought up within the
Christian tradition, and those brought up to be familiar with it,
even though not part of it, do have some concept of providence
based on an acquaintance with the usage of the tradition. This
concept may be vague; it may perhaps be so confused that it
would be better to abandon it, but it provides a starting point.
Thus the analogies that I use may brighten some kind of twilight,
and they may also be checked for adequacy by means of the
understanding we already have. The principal source for this tradition is the scriptures, which are known, often in detail, even by
many who reject their message. Also relevant is later religious
experience and language within the tradition. In all this I am not
making any assumptions about what is true in the order of reality,
but I am accepting the claim that the tradition does give some
initial meaning to the concept of providence.

2. *The analogy of the sun*

In Plato we have already come across the sun as an analogy for
the ultimate being, and this imagery is also found in the Old
Testament when speaking of God,[5] and in the New Testament
when speaking of the face of Christ.[6] Within Judaism and Christianity, because of the emphasis on the sun as a created object,
and because of early fears of idolatry,[7] it was more usual to speak
of God as 'light',[8] but this analogy is obviously similar.

On the positive side there are four features of this analogy that
capture part of the Creator-creature relationship. (1) The sun is,
humanly speaking, virtually changeless in itself; the changes we
observe are due to blockages, e.g. the earth's rotation, eclipses,
our blindness. (2) The sun shines with a steady force, and yet we
experience sudden illuminations, like dawn, or the parting of
clouds. In the use of the analogy this allows for the continuous

activity of God and also for the discontinuity of our experience. (3) We have a certain natural affinity and affection for light, and above all for the source of light. Even the birds have their 'dawn chorus'. (4) The sun, as the source of the light by which we see, does suggest divine initiative or grace. We find this in Plato, and a Christian illustration would be the use of the Psalm 'in thy light shall we see light'.[9]

On the negative side there are three major deficiencies in the analogy. (1) The sun is obviously a physical object, although a very special one. 'Light' in general is less obviously a created 'thing', but there is clearly a sense in which it, too, is part of the physical order. (2) The power of the sun is limited; it could not, for example, shine in Plato's cave. In contrast, the Psalmist observed, 'If I say, Peradventure the darkness shall cover me: then shall my night be turned to day. Yea, the darkness is no darkness with thee, but the night is as clear as the day: the darkness and light to thee are both alike.'[10] (3) The sun, like Plato's Idea of the Good, is impersonal, unaware of and unconcerned with that which it illuminates.

These built-in limitations do not prevent the sun, or the idea of light, from being powerful Christian symbols. One of the best uses, and one that begins to transcend the deficiencies while still using the analogy, is that of John Mason, the seventeenth-century poet. I give it in context.

> Thou art a sea without a shore,
> A sun without a sphere;
> Thy time is now and evermore,
> Thy place is everywhere.[11]

3. The analogy of the wind

So powerful and suggestive is the experience of wind that words for it tend to become words for the profound and subtle concept of spirit. This is due in part to the power and unpredictability of the physical manifestation of wind, and in part to its association with life through breathing, for the ideas of breath and of wind are closely linked.

The use of the Hebrew, *ruach*, in the Old Testament, is a good example of the suggestive force of wind. This can mean the physical power of wind as an agent of God,[12] it can mean the breath of living creatures,[13] and as a derivative from this in post-exilic

times it came to mean the soul of man.[14] Of particular interest for
this study are the cases where *ruach* represents the divine activity.
For example, just before the creation of light we read, 'The spirit
(*ruach*) of God moved upon the face of the waters'.[15] A hero such
as Samson was dramatically empowered when 'the spirit (*ruach*)
of the Lord came mightily upon him'.[16] Another example of interest is Psalm 139, where escape from the *ruach* of God is pro-
claimed as impossible. It goes into the dark (as the quotation in
the last section asserted) and to the uttermost parts of heaven and
hell; hence the rhetorical question, 'Whither shall I go then from
thy spirit?'[17]

In the New Testament the Greek *pneuma* has a similar ambiguity to the Hebrew *ruach*, and is usually used in a way that
demands translation by the word 'spirit'. In John we have a particularly interesting use of wind to represent the power of God.
'The wind blows where it wills, and you hear the sound of it, but
you do not know whence it comes or whither it goes: so it is with
every one who is born of the Spirit.'[18] This passage suggests a
classical four-term analogy. As the unpredictable wind blows the
leaves, so God's spirit enters human hearts.

In some ways this analogy is better than the previous one, for
it seems less tied to a physical object, the sun, even though wind
itself, the movement of air, is perhaps more 'physical' than the
light which comes from the sun. Again, it is easier to think of
wind penetrating the depths of the cave than light, because it can
go round corners. Both wind and light share the idea of immense
power, and can suggest divine initiative, but the analogy of wind
has a dimension of unpredictability that is valuable. It can suggest
'whim' (the wind bloweth where it listeth), and this in turn can
suggest 'will', so that the analogy can evoke the idea of a vast but
personal force.

In order to bring out the last point I want to refer to the actual
experience of a certain aspect of nature. If we look at the surface
of a lake on a windy day we can discern two distinct effects of the
wind. The first is a steady pattern of waves that build up in what
seamen know as the 'fetch'. It is a sort of a rolling motion, with
wave following wave at a fairly predictable height and distance
from each other. But superimposed upon this regular pattern of
waves are sudden gusts or flurries, often coming from odd angles,
which play upon the water. If the regular pattern of waves is not
too big, then this playful-like wind ruffles up the water in its path.

I am inclined to find in this observation a parallel to the dis-

tinction between general and special providence. The steady flow
of wind produces a kind of continuous pressure which does not
determine exactly when each leaf will fall or each wave will roll
but which, in the long run, necessitates certain movements. The
trees will bend away from the prevailing wind, bird migrations
will follow it, and by a corresponding divine 'pressure' evolution
and history move in certain directions. Superimposed upon this
general pattern, which provides a sort of prearranged stage and
backcloth, there are the local flurries, utterly unpredictable, as
are the acts of special providence. These local flurries may be of
crucial importance in the life of an individual, and very occasionally, for some special reason, they may affect a great movement,
as a falling tree, in exceptional circumstances, might divert a river.

Although wind has been a frequent symbol for religious ideas,
I am not aware that any writer has previously used this twofold
activity of wind, but I suggest that this complexity of the human
experience of wind has in fact helped to give it the evocative
power that it possesses. Moreover, the wind, like other examples
from nature, may not just *happen* to be evocative of spiritual
insights. If, like the Christian, one believes in a 'sacramental'
universe, in which the natural order is created not only just to be
there, and to be a suitable environment for man, but also to
reflect in itself something of the beauty of the Creator, then nature
must be full of spiritual lessons. The problem of interpretation
lies in our blindness.

There are two principal shortcomings of the analogy as I have
developed it. First, even though the flurries convey a useful sense
of the unpredictable, they would appear to be capricious rather
than significant. Second, we are still clearly dependent on a physical mechanism, for wind produces all its effects by bombarding
its target with particles of air.

4. *The analogy of the tide*

Let us imagine a seashore with the waves falling upon it under a
continuous but light wind. The motion we see is of countless
waves repeating similar patterns, but each wave is slightly different
from any other. The specific movement of each wave is the result
of several factors, but chiefly of the earth's gravity and the movement of the water's surface brought about by the wind. However,
if we watch the shore for a considerable period of time, then in
addition to the movement of individual waves we shall notice a

general movement. Gradually the water as a whole moves up and down the shore-line on a regular basis, perhaps rising to some forty feet from low tide to high tide, with high tides repeated twice every twenty-five hours. The explanation, of course, is the action of the moon's gravity upon the whole body of water.

This picture affords a good analogy for the activity called general providence, whether this be in terms of the long-run effect of God's activity in the orders of nature, or of man, or of history. It has, as I shall try to show, certain advantages over the model of the steady beam of the sun's light, or the pressure of a regular wind. We can see very clearly in this model how the individual event or person may be unpredictable, and yet the whole sweep of the movement may be predictable and necessary within very narrow limits. The tide will rise forty feet, not forty-one, though perhaps when it comes to millimetres the capacity to predict will cease. When applied to social movements the argument resembles that of Kant, who pointed out that we may predict very accurately how many people will get married in a certain year, although the individual marriages are freely entered upon.[19] In both the tide and the marriage figures there is what might be called a general pressure on the individual units. If there are few units the result is unpredictable, but as the number grows the probability of the predicted outcome increases, until we have a sea, or a population of millions, and then the outcome can be considered certain unless some totally new factor emerges, like an earthquake, or a war.

Superficially there is a certain resemblance in all this to quantum mechanics, where the behaviour of large groups of particles is predictable, but that of the individual particle is not. However, in this latter case, at least one of the reasons for the unpredictability of the individual is the inability to observe it without interfering with it, and this is not parallelled in my analogy, so that I do not want to press this resemblance. Another misleading move would be to liken the activity of the individual waves to the activity of special providence, while the tidal movement represented general providence. This would be a mistake, for a meaningful doctrine of providence must be in the context of activity which is not providential. (This is part of the problem with the idea of universal providence.) Therefore the movement of the individual waves corresponds to the operation of the secondary laws of nature, which must be taken as autonomous, even though they have an ultimate dependence on God's creative and sustaining hand. Hence, while in the wind analogy the realm of the unpredictable was that of special providence, in this analogy of the tide the realm of the unpredictable is that of the individual event or coincidence that arises in nature. General providence is sandwiched, as it were, between two very different kinds of unpredictability, special providence above, depending on an intelligent will, and coincidence below, depending on the autonomous laws of nature.

This analogy can nevertheless be expanded to illustrate something akin to special providence. In the introduction I described how special providence could be regarded as a particular case of general providence, and not as a genuinely separate class of divine activity, although I do not hold that this is always the interpretation of special providence that ought to be adopted.

The extension of the analogy is as follows. In some situations the force of steady tidal pressure produces dramatic results. On certain tides, an enormous wave known as a 'bore' travels up a river that runs into a tidal estuary. To the uninitiated the sudden appearance of this bore can be both astonishing and terrifying. To those who know the pressures the coming of the bore is predictable, just as those who know the pressures on a bridge, and the mathematics of catastrophe theory, can predict when the bridge will collapse. So we have the appearance of a radical and surprising discontinuity, but the explanation does not in fact require the introduction of any strange new factors.

Over all, then, this analogy suggests that general providence is like the tidal movement. The moon's gravity draws the water, rather like Aristotle's *eros* draws the inner spheres, both producing a necessary and repeated pattern of movement. Thus, hypothetically, every thousandth star has a medium-sized and temperate planet which, under certain laws which result from a continuous divine pressure, brings forth first life, then conscious life, and finally self-conscious life. Further, this same pressure builds up huge forces in certain situations which result in sudden and, to the uninformed, inexplicable phenomena, like an earthquake, or the conversion of a Paul. If this analogy is alleged to be sufficient for the characterization of all aspects of providence, then special providence must be interpreted after this model.

On the negative side, in addition to the reductionist account of personal divine action, this analogy suffers from two major limitations. First, the force of the moon's gravity is in fact of the same order as that of the earth, whose gravity is part of the explanation of the local motion of individual waves. Therefore we do not have a sufficiently radical distinction between primary and secondary causality, to put it in Thomistic terms. Second, and closely related to this first problem, the moon is very obviously a physical object. Nevertheless, the idea of gravity has some advantages over both light and wind as symbols for divine action. It has less physical associations than either, and is more penetrating. Gravity can enter the dark cave, even when the door is shut against the wind. We may be able to counter-balance the force of gravity, but we cannot stop its entrance, even with the most massive screens. It is a good way of illustrating the searching power of God as described in Psalm 139.

5. *The space-time analogy*

The analogies I have explored so far are concerned with the relationship of God to the created order, and they all have reference to the question 'How does God effect change or movement, while he himself is changeless?' One important answer that has been given is that he does not effect change, because there is no real change, only the illusion of change. The fourth analogy is an attempt to characterize this position, and although what it suggests must, for the most part, be rejected by the tradition that we are considering, I think that it is useful to include it, partly by way of contrast, and partly because within certain limits it has an application to the concept of providence.

Let us suppose that we record the change in the surface that we see set out spatially before us. My desk displays a radical discontinuity as my eye moves across it. That lump is my diary, then there is a flat piece of table-top, then a paper, more flat surface, and so on. On a larger scale I see a similar discontinuity if I look at the scene outside my window. But, it might be argued, these appearances of discontinuity are only local. If I were to take a position in deep space the scene before me would present uniformity in all directions, stars, nebulae, galaxies repeated over and over again. Locally there would be immense variation, for 'star differs from star in glory',[20] but the further I stand back, as it were, the more uniform the appearance. If I were a giant, for whom the galaxies were grains of sand, then I would be wading through an infinite and never-changing desert.

Of course this suggestion is predicated on a theory of the universe, the 'steady state' theory, that is disputable. On some views there is a radical discontinuity in the universe even on the grand, macrocosmic level. However, for the purpose of exploiting the

analogy, we can take the 'steady state' theory as a provisional
model of the universe. In a sense, then, the argument goes, there
is no significant change. The universe as a whole presents a vast
homogeneity. (A similar argument might be presented with respect to the microcosmic level.)

The situation regarding spatial change is exactly paralleled by
temporal change. The particular leaf in front of me yellows and
crumbles away; there is radical discontinuity. But then I move to
the forest and the picture is more complex. Over three months
there is the change of season, and the appearance of the forest is
much altered, but over twelve months the appearance is very
similar, only some trees have fallen and the rest are a little bigger.
If I stand back in time much more, and see the forest over the
centuries, then the individual trees cease to be significant. There
is just the forest, and the changing seasons are a local phenomenon, like the flickering of a light bulb as the current oscillates.
But, one may object, the forest eventually dies, at the next ice-
age, or the next round of human destruction of nature. The response to this is to step back further still, like our giant in the
galactic sand, and then, within the model of the universe that we
are working with, there is again an incredible sameness to the
universe. Individual stars come and go, like the flickering seasons,
but that is irrelevant if our time scale is big enough. To pursue
the desert analogy, individual grains of sand get ground down in
time, but their matter becomes the basis for new bits of sand, just
as the energy of a dying star eventually becomes the raw material
for another star. So my giant wades through an endless and eternal
desert of sand. Now take away the giant, and we have no change
except for local motion, a local motion that gives to the tiny and
insignificant observer the illusion of change.

This may not be well expressed, but I have tried to capture
what has for a long time been a powerful and influential view of
the universe, a view that is essentially monistic, in which all things
can be said to be ultimately one, and in this abiding unity there
is no real change. Monism has a great appeal, and it is not surprising that many religious systems embrace a world view along
the lines of the picture I have drawn. Even some versions of
Christianity tend towards it.

It should be noted that this fourth analogy is not strictly a
four-term analogy, and this is so precisely because it is not really
a model for divine action, in a theistic sense, but a denial of it. In
a monistic system you cannot say, 'As A is to B, so God is to C',

because God is not a being that is external to the universe. The analogy is rather, 'the changeless face of space is like the changeless face of time'.

However, I claimed earlier that this analogy had an application for the theist, and it is this. So far as the universal order of nature is concerned, considered in isolation from man, the picture may be convincing, and even helpful for some theists. This is especially the case if we accept Aquinas' claim that there can be no valid metaphysical argument to show that the universe has any temporal beginning.[21] Where there must be radical discontinuity for the theist, and especially for the Christian, is in the world of persons, and in the derivative realm of history. Individual persons are born, mature, and die: here is radical discontinuity. If these persons persist in some way after death, and even if they had existed before for an endless time backwards, which is the case in some reincarnational views, so long as there is such a thing as salvation, and/or moral and spiritual progress, there is still radical discontinuity. The argument from size, reached by looking at the universe from the point of view of an inter-galactic giant, now becomes quite irrelevant. Persons are neither large nor small in the sense that particles or galaxies are large and small. Their manifestations as bodies do of course have spatial properties, but persons are persons. Like numbers, they are, in an important sense, space-transcending.[22]

The theist is therefore bound to reject my space-time analogy, or systems that amount to it, when the claim is made that they picture the whole of reality. Perhaps he cannot prove that the analogy is false – indeed it is not clear what would count as proof in such an undertaking – but he can prove that it is inconsistent with a cardinal emphasis in his tradition, in which persons are given a central importance. This is true, in turn, because for the theist God is personal, or more strictly *the* person, the prime analogue of personality.

Once again, part of my argument in later chapters has emerged, namely that any theological position that can claim genuine roots in the biblical and Christian traditions is bound to hold a doctrine of a personal God, and a corresponding doctrine of special providence in order to make this view coherent.

6. *The analogy of human action*

One of the chief difficulties in representing divine action is that if there is a God, in the Judaeo-Christian sense, then he has no body. Yet most analogies for divine action, like that of the sun or the tide, depend upon reference to a physical object as their source. We have, however, one example of a source of movement which, it might be argued, altogether avoids this problem, namely the human mind. We will something that involves bodily movement, and immediately there is movement. The word 'immediately' is perhaps misleading because we do know part of the mechanism. My arm moves because the muscles contract, the muscles contract because of a sort of electrical current that travels down the nerves, and it may be possible to go one step further, but then we come to a blank. All mechanical analogies seem to be inadequate; the mind just has the ability to initiate the energy flow on which the movement depends.

This, at least, is the account given by many people, but it is hotly disputed by others. Hobbes, for example, and many materialists who follow him in essentials, see man as a kind of engine, so that ultimately bodily movement is to be explained like every other movement. 'Thinking' is the name we give to a special kind of local motion that takes place in the brain, and is initiated as a response to outside stimuli. 'Will' is the last act of the deliberative process, and as such it is an example of interior motion which is perfectly capable of setting off a causal chain, ending with external, bodily motion.[23]

However, this account of human thought seems totally implausible to others, even when couched in the much more subtle language of modern exponents of a body-mind identity. Even if every thought is associated with an electrical or chemical process in the brain, simply to identify them seems to be a mistake. This may be asserted even if electrical and chemical processes are the whole originating cause of my thoughts – a supposition which is by no means established. Congruously, my sensation of redness is caused by my perception of a certain wavelength of light, but my perception of redness is not the same thing as the light wave. It is an internal sensation that demands new categories of language to describe.

It is beyond the scope of this essay to dig deeply into the difficult subject of the relationship of the mind to the body, but in order to justify an exploration of the present analogy it is necessary to

point out that there is a large and respectable body of opinion
which rejects any behaviouristic account of mind. This rejection
is not based on a desire to preserve some kind of orthodoxy, but
on the claim that the reductionist account fails to do justice to the
complexity of human experience and behaviour, especially as
these are exhibited in language, though it is also true that those
within the religious tradition that I am concerned with would have
added reasons for being suspicious of the reductionist account.
This appeal to authority in no way proves the truth of my own
position, but it does demonstrate that there is no *prima facie*
reason for accepting the reductionist account either. Authorities
prove nothing in this kind of dispute, but a provisional agnosticism
about the issue, reached through an awareness of the controversy,
can allow us to entertain the present analogy as a possible source
for insight.

The analogy that I am exploring may be put as follows. 'As the
mind of man initiates movement by an act of will, so God causes
movement in the universe by his will.' It must be noted that
consideration of this analogy does not necessitate acceptance of
a complete mind-body dualism of the kind associated with Plato
or Descartes. For such philosophers, the true person was identified with a soul that could exist without any kind of body. Many
thinkers, however, have defended a much less radical dualism,
which accepts a close relationship between the spiritual side of
man, and his body, while maintaining their irreducibility. This
kind of dualism is not necessarily committed to the view that the
person could exist in any significant sense without a body. However, it could still be proper to speak of a person manifesting
himself in and through his body. An able defence of such a view
is presented in two books by H. D. Lewis, and they contain a
particularly valuable critique of Ryle's *Concept of Mind*.[24]

The advantage of this analogy is that we seem at last to have
got away from the series of physical models with their suggestion
of a God who operates a sort of celestial lever that offsets other
forces and brings new ones into play, which is to make God a
cause alongside other causes, and ultimately an object, albeit a
very special one, within the universe. But has anything really been
gained, it may be asked, because we seem to have replaced one
obscurity by another? If there is a God, we know nothing of *how*
he effects change, just as if there is a mind which cannot be
reduced to the purely physical, we know nothing of *how* this mind

effects change. So the only thing in common between divine action and human action is obscurity!

If the analogy is held to illuminate the mechanism by which providence works, then I think that this would be a just criticism. However, this analogy may have another aim, namely that of suggesting that there is a correspondence between the mysterious way in which we are able to initiate bodily movement, and the mysterious way in which God can effect change in nature. It can be argued that the human mind does have this power without simply being another lever in a chain of levers, and since the Christian believes that man is made in the image of God, this human experience may be taken as a possible clue to the divine activity. But it is not so much an indication of *how* God operates as an indication *that* he operates.

This argument may be fortified by the familiar claim that it is in fact from the observation of our own power to initiate movement that we get the idea of causal power in the first place, an argument found especially in Locke and Reid.[25] On this view our conception of the causal powers of the physical order is derivative from this prior conception of human causation. Moreover, their operation, ultimately, is as obscure as that of the causal powers of the mind. We can explain the moon's tidal power in terms of gravity, but we cannot yet explain gravity itself. If at some time in the future we can explain gravity in terms of a more primordial force, say that of electric charge, then this in turn will need to be explained. Thus with all causal explanations we are bound to end up in due course with a statement like 'This is the nature of things', or 'This just is the property of this particle', and so on.

The inevitable limits to any explanatory process highlight the fact that a considerable part of the adequacy of an explanation is psychological. We feel that a puzzling occurrence is explained when it is made to fit into a general pattern with which we are familiar; then we will tend to be satisfied, and not to ask further questions. The apparently strong tree fell on the roof, and we ask 'Why?' We find that it was rotten inside, and then the odd event is explained. The tree had not the strength to maintain its position under the forces of wind and gravity. It would seem odd, in most contexts, to ask further 'But why does the force of gravity follow the inverse square law?', because we live in a world where the first 'Why?' can often be answered, and in which we may need to find the answer for practical reasons, but in which the second

'Why?' can almost never be answered, and we can get by perfectly well without answering it.

This is not the whole story of what it is to be an explanation, for there must be some rational grounds for an explanation to be a good explanation, like coherence with other explanations, and this coherence is not a purely psychological matter. Nevertheless, the discussion brings out the point that there is something misleading in the assumption that there is something mysterious about the explanation of human action, unless man is ultimately reducible to a complex machine, and no mystery about other kinds of activity. It is misleading to call obscure or mysterious that with which we are perfectly familiar; so we might argue that there is nothing obscure either about the nature of gravity, or about minds initiating movement, for we observe examples of both countless times each day. There is obscurity at another level of question, a question about how gravity, or how minds, can have these properties, but with this sort of question the honest person will admit his ignorance.

In the light of all this, what value can we find in the suggested analogy, 'As the mind of man initiates movement by an act of will, so God causes movement in the universe by his will'? Three positive features of this analogy come to mind. (1) As I have already stressed, we are beginning to escape from the source of movement being likened to a physical object. Minds, except for out-and-out materialists, are not objects in space. (2) We have a variety of mind-controlled actions, some continuous and virtually automatic, like breathing, and others deliberate, like signing my name. These modes of action can be likened to general and special providence respectively. (3) We have in human action an example of movement that is neither coincidence nor miracle. A coincidence requires only the laws of secondary causality to explain fully what happened, while a miracle demands an explanation other than that offered by these secondary laws. Both providential action and human action occupy a position somewhere in between, and because this intermediate position is so hard to characterize, there is a tendency to reduce both of them to something else. Thus the materialist reduces all human action to purely natural laws, and the nominalist reduces all God's action to miracle.

The situation here has an interesting parallel in the problem of rival accounts of the inspiration of scripture, and the issue is in fact related to the problem under discussion. The extreme positions are: (1) the scriptures are purely human creations, inspired only in the sense that a materialist might say that works of art are inspired. (2) The scriptures are literally dictated by God, so that the only room for error is in scribal transmission when words get miscopied. Both these views have a certain charming simplicity and consistency, but many Christians are happy with neither account. They prefer to take the risk of attempting to discover an intermediate position that is much harder to describe, but which is more in harmony with the complexity of human experience. In this intermediate position the inspiration is neither coincidence nor pure miracle. There could be an explanation of what prompted the human writer to write as he did, but this would have to include the writer's awareness of God.

Similarly, both human and providential action have natural explanations, which from one point of view might be complete. I signed my name by certain muscular actions, and God drove back the sea by a strong east wind, but in both cases this may not be the whole story. (One recalls here Socrates' irritation with the suggestion that the explanation for his position was in terms of the mechanics of his body.[26]) In the case of providence, how do we know that this is not the whole story? Strictly speaking, we cannot *know*, for the religious interpretation is a matter of faith, not of knowledge, but this does not mean that the interpretation must be groundless, like a wild leap into the unknown.

To return to the analogy. Over against the three strong points which the analogy enjoys, there is one serious weakness. The mind has a unique relationship to the body. Although, in my view, they cannot be identified, I must manifest myself through a body; and if there are further levels of existence, the same will presumably be true. Therefore I can be said to 'have' a body, even though not in the same way that I 'have' a wrist-watch, or even a scar. But within the tradition I am exploring the physical universe is not God's body in *any* sense. Such an idea is not without its attraction, and is endorsed in some forms of pantheism, but the idea of a Creator God, complete and changeless in himself, is clearly incompatible with this view. Moreover, if the universe were God's body, the analogy we are working with would not be so much an analogy as an example of divine action. It is just because God is separate from, and uniquely different from, any created thing that we have to grope for one analogy after another. But if man is truly made in the image of God, then this analogy of human action has a special appropriateness as a model for providential action.

7. *The mechanism of divine action*

According to the theistic tradition, God is active in the created
order, but it will be apparent from what I have written so far that
I do not think that a clear account of the mechanism by which
God operates can be given. I agree with a recent thesis on the
problem of providence that this is basically an area for agnosticism.[27] There are two reasons for this. First, there is the unique-
ness and transcendent nature of God according the whole theistic
tradition. This is perhaps most strongly emphasized in the Koran,
but it is also a persistent feature of the Judaic and Christian
scriptures. We may recall, for example, the emphasis on transcendence in the book of Job, especially where God speaks
through the whirlwind,[28] and the Psalmist's prayer to the God
who 'deckest thyself with light as it were with a garment'.[29] This
theme is well expressed also in another part of the poem by John
Mason already quoted from:

> How great a being, Lord, is thine,
> Which doth all beings keep!
> Thy knowledge is the only line
> To sound so vast a deep.

Second, as I have already suggested, the very concern with the
'mechanism' of God's action may be systematically misleading,
for it already assumes a false analogy. The situation is similar in
the free will debate, where so many accounts of how human
decisions are made picture the deciding and willing processes as
if they were like the operation of scales, with weights balanced on
either side until the balance necessarily goes down one way or the
other. But such imagery is question-begging, for the use of the
scales analogy assumes a mechanistic and deterministic position,
and does not entertain the possibility of a radical freedom in which
there is a decision as to how far to weigh a given factor, and in
which this element of decision cannot in turn be described in
balance terms without destroying its very point. For the Christian
tradition, man, in this matter at least, is not like a machine.[30]

Thus instead of discussing the mechanism of God's action, could
we simply say that according to the tradition, he wills, and that
his will is effective, though we cannot say how?

This is too short an answer for the intelligent theist, because
we then have no means of making some distinctions that are
essential for any understanding of the concept of providence. We

need to be able to distinguish in principle between four kinds of activity: (1) 'ordinary' natural activities, including what is properly called 'coincidence'; (2) the activity of general providence; (3) the activity of special providence; (4) the miraculous.

Within the Christian tradition all four of these activities are manifestations of God's will in one way or another. The first comprises God's work as creator, sustainer, and as final cause – or as the creator of an inherent final causality. However, when we seek explanations within the ordinary run of nature, we put on one side, as it were, any knowledge we have of God's action under these headings. God's very purpose in creating this order was to allow it to be treated as autonomous, except when treated as a whole. The other three kinds of activity are claimed to bear some kind of witness to God's activity, but in different ways. Number three is the most difficult to handle conceptually, because we seem in most need of a convincing analogy. General providence can be likened to a general 'pressure', according to the tidal analogy, a pressure which is superimposed upon the immediate forces at work on each particle of nature. Miracle can be likened to a deliberate interference with the general operation of a process. But how is special providence to be characterized? The fifth analogy contrasted deliberate human action, like signing my name, with semi-automatic human action, like breathing, but the deliberate action here, while most appropriate as a model for special providence, is not clearly contrasted with miracle.

I have suggested how events which fall under special providence should be identified from the human point of view. It is their frequency, plus their significance, plus the fact that they seem individually to be part of the natural process. It is impossible to prove that any one event is not a coincidence, and whether or not we believe that it is a coincidence will depend on our overall world view, for the most part established prior to the event. But either for an individual, or for a closely knit group, a series of events can become the appropriate verification of the personal hypothesis I described in the introduction. In principle, therefore, events that fall under special providence can be identified.

It follows, however, that if in principle these events can be identified by humans, this is possible only because there is in fact some intrinsic difference between the nature of these events that fall under special providence, and other events, such as genuine coincidence and miracle. Otherwise, our separating out of these events refers only to our psychological concerns, and not to the

nature of things as they are. So, in order for there to be a special
providence, in the sense that I have claimed that the tradition
demands, from God's point of view there must be a real distinction
between deliberate manifestations of his will and general manifestations of his will, and also, within deliberate manifestations of
his will, between those that operate through natural powers alone
(i.e. special providence) and those that go beyond them, (i.e. the
miraculous).

The sort of position that belief in a special providence requires
is well expressed in the work of Sherlock already referred to: 'The
ordinary government of nature [that is, providential guidance as
opposed to intervention by miracle] does not signify to act without
it, or to overrule its powers, but to steer and guide its motions,
to serve the wise ends of his providence in the government of
mankind.' He goes on to explain that fire, water, wind, etc. have
their natural powers, but 'when and where the rains shall fall',
etc., 'this God keeps in his own power, and can govern, without
altering the standing laws of nature'.[31]

This position raises considerable difficulties which I shall turn
to in the next chapter, but I contend that something along these
lines must be said if there is to be a meaningful doctrine of special
providence. For providence, under both its aspects, there has to
be possible a class of events which are examples of the working
of natural laws, and yet in which God is somehow 'steering' the
outcome; otherwise, there is no middle ground between ordinary
nature and the miraculous. I shall argue, that despite very real
difficulties, this notion of 'steering' nature can help both to characterize providence in general, and to clarify the distinction between general and special providence.

IV

Providence in the Order of Nature

1. Taking stock

The first three chapters have provided a basic grammar for the concept of providence, and in a limited way we now know how the term should be used. A summary of this grammar can be given as follows.

In a broad sense providence can refer to some or all of the six kinds of divine activity discussed in the introduction, but in a stricter sense it refers to only two of these, which can be classed as general and special providence. Providence, by itself, may refer to either of these categories, or to the two of them taken together.

General providence must not be confused with universal providence, which is a particular interpretation of divine activity, commonly found in some schools of Christianity and in popular Islam. The latter assumes a general determinism of all events by God that cannot, in my judgment, be accommodated to the mainstream Christian tradition. A consequence of this rejection of universal providence is that providential activity can be contrasted with non-providential activity.[1] This important point must be stated carefully. Only some events are held to fall under special providence, so that here there is a clear contrast with non-providential events. However, there is a sense in which all events fall under general providence. Nevertheless, this does not refer to the determination of particular events, but rather to something analogous to a general or tidal pressure, exerting a long-run influence that may be seen as determining the general pattern that emerges.

It might be said, therefore, that general providence is *one* of the factors that goes towards the over all determining of every event, but this must not be taken to imply that it is another physical factor, to be placed alongside factors such as gravity, wind, temperature, etc. General providence can be significant only if the possibility is entertained that an intelligent God can influence events by his consistent *use of such physical factors*. His will is then a factor, but of a different order, with the result that, with the exception of the miraculous, adequate explanations can be given for all individual events without any mention of God. This use of an 'adequate explanation' is based on the concept of a natural order with its own internal coherence; it cannot mean a 'complete explanation', as the religious man would understand that phrase, for this would have to include the providential activity. Thus the concept of providence is linked with a concept of nature, a concept that is separate from it, but which is also the context within which it gathers its meaning.

Not only must general providence be contrasted with universal providence, and with the ordinary working of nature; it must also be contrasted with creation. When the idea of creation is enriched in order to include the sustaining power of God, and the activity of final causality, meaning a principle that is ordering the activities of all natural things from within, then the distinction begins to get blurred. Nevertheless, there is still a difference of emphasis, since general providence suggests the intelligent planning and governing of events in a continuing way. However, some interpretations of creation, with an emphasis on a 'continuing creation', effect a merging of the ideas of creation and of general providence.[2]

Special providence shares with general providence the idea of intelligent control, and of nature being 'steered' in order to fulfil the purposes of God, but it refers to specific events rather than to general movements, and is held to mirror the specific decisions of a personal God. Events that fall under special providence have to be distinguished from specific events that fall under the ordinary running of nature, including those that we should call 'coincidences', and also from miracles. 'Coincidence', it should be noted, is a legitimate term within the view that I am describing, and refers to the individual, unexpected event that is not deliberately planned by man or God, but just allowed to happen under the ordinary laws of nature. Special providence refers to events that lie in a sense between coincidence and miracle. They are under God's direction, but do not involve the overruling of nature.

This clarification serves to focus the peculiar problem that modern man has with the concept of providence, for it must be asked,

'How can there be events that are part of nature, and yet that are also instances of divine intervention?' The issue might also be put this way: 'Is not to steer nature ultimately to interfere with it, so that events that are not only psychologically significant, but also significant because of some divine initiative that brought them about, must be miracles? What room is there for a further class of providential events?'

Given the difficulty of explaining how there can be a class of events that falls under providence I need now to carry out the promise made in the introduction, namely to explore what the concept of providence can mean within our contemporary understanding of nature, of man, and of history. In the rest of this chapter I turn to the question of providence in the natural order, meaning by that the inorganic and organic context for human life, including our own physical bodies, but excluding the special problems raised by the existence of intelligent, self-conscious life.

2. Sherlock's account of providence

At the end of the last chapter we began to explore Sherlock's account of how God 'steers' nature without overruling it, governing the times and places where it will rain, or where other natural phenomena will occur, in order to reward, to punish, and generally to direct the affairs of this world. He goes on to marshal an impressive array of biblical passages to show that this is how the matter should be viewed. For example, he quotes Amos' declaration, 'I caused it to rain upon one city, and caused it not to rain upon another city.'[3]

But there is an obvious objection to this argument. If the rain is to have its natural powers, but God is to choose when and where it rains, surely this is not to let the wind and certain other natural agencies have *their* natural powers? When and where it rains is not decided by the intrinsic properties of rain, but we have good reason to think that it is determined by the intrinsic properties of a series of other natural factors, such as the evaporation of the oceans, the temperature, wind-direction, etc. How can God 'steer' these processes and at the same time respect all natural powers?

This difficulty is not avoided by giving a purely empirical account of natural processes that abandons the notion of 'powers' in nature, and analyses causation in the way that Hume advocated. Laws of nature are then explained purely in terms of our observation of constant conjunction, and the only necessity involved is a psychological one concerning our expectations. However, within such a view the issue that I am concerned with simply reappears in a slightly different form; for we now have to ask, 'How can God be said to "steer" nature if there is no observable departure from the regular laws of nature?' In fact there has been a strong reaction to Hume's analysis, and to those that resemble it, and some modern philosophers of science, such as Harré and Madden, are anxious to return to the concept of 'powers' in nature, though without some of the metaphysical implications that the term formerly held.[4] This reaction to Humean philosophy is, in my view, a welcome return to a more adequate understanding of the order of nature, and is more congruous with a Christian philosophy of primary and secondary causality; but whichever analysis one favours the issue under discussion remains.

Sherlock does not appear to be sensitive to the issue here. He argues, with much plausibility, that 'it is impossible to give any tolerable account of texts as these', or of the very notion of God's rule in the world, unless 'God keeps the springs of nature in his own hand, and turns them as he pleases,'[5] but he does not explain how this is compatible with respecting nature and not overruling it.

At this point in the discussion it is once again vital to tread carefully. It can easily appear as if I am starting to revert to a 'God of the gaps' picture of God's activity, an approach against which C. A. Coulson has wisely warned us. But in order to have an adequate doctrine of providence, it is not enough to say with Coulson, 'Either God is in the whole of Nature, with no gaps, or He's not there at all.'[6] I agree that the Christian must say this, but a coherent doctrine of providence must also make some distinctions about how God is related to the world. The claim that God is somehow 'in' all things must be supplemented by an account of the different ways in which God is active, otherwise the implication is either that God directly controls everything, as in the doctrine of universal providence, or that he is some vague cosmic force, akin to a principle of final causality. The statement 'God is in all things' does not explain how the Christian can believe both in a personal God and in a significant order of nature.

Sherlock's suggestion is to liken God's activity to that of the human artist, who, without changing the nature of things, by a 'skilful application of causes' produces what unguided nature could never produce. In an analogous way God has subjected all natures to his guidance.[7]

Before exploring this suggestion further I propose to review some recent responses to the question of the nature of providence.

3. *Some recent accounts of the nature of divine action*

(a) *Sub-atomic action.* One suggestion for the location of divine action in nature has been prompted by modern physics, and especially by Heisenberg's uncertainty principle. The physicist W. G. Pollard, in his *Chance and Providence*,[8] starts from this principle. He bases his case on the claim that 'the ultimate as well as present characteristic mode of scientific explanation in all fields is statistical', and argues that this is the result, not of our temporary lack of knowledge, but of the very nature of things.[9] This he sees as a promising background for any account of providence, for he urges that it is a requirement of any account of providence that the world have many possibilities open to it.[10] There are, therefore, chance and accident in the shaping of the world's history, and these provide the opportunity for God's activity. 'The Christian sees the chances and accidents of history as the very warp and woof of the fabric of providence which God is ever weaving.'[11] However, providence is not 'an added non-physical force in nature whose operation produces discernible and verifiable empirical consequences by means of which it can be objectively established'.[12] The result is that the indeterminacy of contemporary physics does not in any way demonstrate providence, but it allows for it, and the Christian 'insight'[13] will be able to detect it in the dynamic reality of life.

There is a great deal of interesting material in this book, and Pollard is certainly sensitive to the basic difficulty with which I am wrestling, for he is anxious to see how God can be said to produce significant events without violating any scientific law.[14] Nevertheless, there are three major problems that Pollard's position raises. First, it does look very much like a sophisticated version of the 'God of the gaps' approach, for providence works at the sub-atomic level where the outcome is not predictable for man. However, I do not think that this is an overpowering objection. In this case the gaps are of a very different kind from those exemplified in the classical retreats with which Coulson was concerned, when the inexplicable was held to be the area of God's work, and God gradually receded as more and more became explained. The gaps involved in the explanation of sub-atomic particles are infinite and all-pervasive, at least within the context of the view of physics that Pollard upholds. A second problem concerns the evident commitment to the view that God's government through his influence on sub-atomic particles is total, and this seems to imply the objectionable doctrine of universal providence.[15] However, I think that Pollard's view, in essentials, could be restated in a way that avoids this implication. The third, and most significant problem, is that Pollard's approach does not in fact advance any view as to how God influences events, only that the nature of the physical universe does not rule out such influence. A location for divine influence is suggested, but no real progress is made with regard to its manner.

(b) *Action at the personal level.* A very different view is that which banishes God from direct action on nature as such (unless we refer to the actual creation of nature), but allows for God's action on persons, and through persons on the order of nature.

Some support for this position can be found in the New Testament if certain passages are emphasized. In the Old Testament we have seen that *ruach* could mean either 'wind' or 'spirit', and when it meant 'wind' this was very much the agent of God. In the New Testament there are indications that the physical order was beginning to be seen as having some independence, and accordingly *anemos*, the word usually used for 'wind', does not indicate 'spirit' as does *pneuma*. *Anemos* seems to be an independent agent,[16] and on at least one occasion it appears to have hampered the spread of the gospel.[17] It was still held to be under God's control, and we may recall the famous passage when Jesus is claimed to have stilled the wind,[18] but this does not alter the fact that the main thrust of Jesus' message was not so much in terms of changing the physical environment as in changing the inner lives of people. Another New Testament passage that invites a similar emphasis is Paul's suggestion that the whole created order 'has been groaning in travail together until now . . . as we wait for adoption'.[19] This suggests that change in the physical order is bound up with change in man's spiritual condition, and that the former will be transformed only through the latter.

However, I do not want to put too much emphasis on these passages, for there is no doubt that the New Testament writers would not have wished to confine God's activity to the spiritual realm, while some modern writers would do just that. The main basis for such a position is the separation of levels of existence, especially the physical and the personal, together with the claim that God, as personal saviour, works at the personal level. An influential version of such a view is found in Christian existentialism of the kind exemplified by Bultmann in his *Jesus Christ and Mythology*.[20] Bultmann sees the physical order as rigidly determined, along the lines of Kant's phenomenal world, for this he believes to be demanded both by an adequate view of science and by the requirements of ordinary life.[21] Therefore God cannot act directly in nature in such a way as to make a difference, though there can be a sort of providence that arises in the way we see events when they become the opportunity for God's self-disclosure.

Bultmann does not want to banish the supernatural altogether from the Bible; he wants rather to 'demythologize' it, that is, to reinterpret it so that its true function is to confront us with a personal God who can transform us. 'God as acting does not refer to an event which can be perceived by me without myself being drawn into the event as into God's action.'[22]

This position raises a number of obvious problems. First, it certainly departs in large measure from the mainstream Christian tradition when it denies that God can affect the natural order directly. This departure is not an argument against his position, but it indicates that acceptance of his position should be seen as drastically modifying the concept of providence. Nevertheless, in Chapter VII I shall suggest that one of the alternatives open to the rational mind is an interpretation of providence that is similar to Bultmann's.

Another problem concerns Bultmann's rigid separation of the worlds of nature and of persons, together with his view of nature as a totally determined system, which now seems somewhat dated. However, we should still consider the suggestion that God works only through personal encounter, for a view very similar to Bultmann's can be expounded which avoids his controversial view of the natural order. We could say, for example, that personal encounters are historical events in time (which Bultmann denies), and we could perhaps be agnostic about whether God *could* act in nature as such, insisting simply that the appropriate and typical sphere of divine activity is personal, and that nature becomes changed indirectly as persons who have been changed then change nature. The dry desert becomes farmland when changed persons transform it by their endeavours. If we favour an approach along these lines, can we be said to have made any progress over the question of how God 'steers' the world?

Superficially the answer is yes, because many people seem to have less difficulty with the idea that God can influence minds than with the idea that he can directly influence physical matter. This will appear even more plausible to some if we stress the Whiteheadean view that God persuades rather than commands, for it is much easier to think of him seeking to persuade persons than matter. Nevertheless, there are many difficulties with positions of this kind.

For example, there is still the suggestion of a radical dualism between spirit and body, for the claim is that the person is not part of the natural order. Does this mean that he inhabits his own body in a way reminiscent of the theories of Plato and Descartes? If so, then, as suggested in Chapter III, the problem of describing the mechanism by which God changes the world is replaced by the equal problem of describing how our minds change the world, including our own bodies. If it is simply asserted that they just do so, as a matter of daily experience, though we do not know how, why should not the traditionalist simply say that God somehow changes things, though again we do not know how?

I think that there are possible answers to this charge of dualism. For example, it might be claimed that man is a creature that is *sui generis*, and unlike anything else in the world that we have so far experienced, who combines in himself attributes of two different categories, the physical and the personal, so that he acts as a kind of mediator between them. However, it is clear that, although a case can be made for the claim that providence works either always, or typically, at the level of persons, this claim, if established, would not remove the problem of the mechanism of God's activity; it would simply relocate it. The grounds for an existentialist-type position are not, in other words, its success in dissolving the present problem, but its attraction as an account of how man in fact experiences the divine. This conclusion is strengthened if we question the assumption that there is less mystery about how God influences persons than about how he influences matter. If God produces wave motions in the brain we are back at the suggestion that he is producing physical effects. If we speak of telepathy we are not only speaking about a phenomenon the existence of which is still under dispute, but we also have no knowledge of the processes involved.

It follows that existentialist approaches make an interesting suggestion as to the location of providential activity, a suggestion that is to be contrasted with that of Pollard, but they do not provide an answer to the puzzle concerning how God can 'steer' the world without interfering with it.

(c) *The principle of synchronicity.* Since the time of Jung's essay, 'Synchronicity: An Acausal Principle',[23] there has been considerable discussion of his claim that contemporary events are linked by a kind of parallelism. Jung's views were formed in part by the influence of the biologist, Paul Kammerer, who was especially interested in the repetition of apparent coincidences and spoke of 'laws of seriality',[24] and in part by his own observation and experiments with coincidence and the paranormal. Jung was impressed by a succession of coincidences, both in his own life and in that of many of his patients, and found himself compelled to speak of 'meaningful coincidences'[25] in a way that is reminiscent of the significant events that I described during the introduction as the main source for belief in special providence. Jung was also convinced of the genuineness of many of the experimental results concerned with ESP and telekinesis, arrived at by Rhine and others, and he linked these as well with his principle. He described the principle in a number of rather baffling ways, including 'the occurrence of meaningful coincidence in time'[26] and insisted that this principle was not to be seen as another causal factor, alongside those uncovered in scientific investigations, but as an *acausal* factor, that had more in common with ancient and holistic ways of looking at the universe. But at the same time he insisted that the presence of this principle was a conclusion drawn from *empirical* premises.[27]

A view essentially similar to that of Jung was put forward by the eminent physicist Wolfgang Pauli,[28] who collaborated with Jung on this matter, and more recently by Arthur Koestler. Koestler, too, wants to stress the acausal nature of the principle of synchronicity, and criticizes both Jung and Pauli for falling into the trap of trying to give pseudo-causal explanations for a principle that is necessarily of a completely different category.[29]

Much of this looks highly relevant to the study of providence, but for reasons that I have already indicated, I think that it is unwise to make a close connection between physical research and problems relating to providence. The main relevance of psychical research is not through an ability to give some insight into the mechanism of providential action, but through the way in which it challenges us to broaden our picture of the universe, and to be

sceptical about theories that do less than justice to the great
variety and complexity of human experience. The inadequacy of
the clockwork model then becomes clearer. Like contemporary
physics, psychical research suggests that the universe is both
stranger than we imagine, and stranger than we can imagine.

I am pleading here for agnosticism, in the strict sense of the
term, with regard to the fundamental nature of the universe.
Fortunately one of the things that rational reflection can achieve,
and especially philosophical reflection on the presuppositions of
our thinking, is the exposure of absolutist knowledge claims. This
is the context in which I have been inviting the reader to entertain
the possibility of a universe in which it could be meaningful to
speak of providence.

To return to Jung's principle of synchronicity: what we have
here is not a clue to the mechanism of divine action, but yet
another possibility with regard to the location of divine action, in
a universe that is not simply the result of empirical laws. The
possibility is to be entertained that a thought, or wish, or inten-
tion, with regard to an object, may be related to the production
of that object somewhere in the universe.

In putting the issue thus I may seem to have misunderstood
Jung's insistence that he is speaking of an *acausal* principle, for
behind my suggestion is the notion that in some way the thought,
etc., is *productive* of the result. But this is precisely how I think
that the principle of synchronicity should be viewed if it is to be
intelligible, and if the empirical basis for it that Jung alleges is
sufficient to warrant its consideration at all. In a recent article,
the psychologist John Beloff has argued along these lines.[30] Jung
was wrong, he argues, to contrast the synchronous with the causal.
Under the conceptual framework within which most people operate there cannot be any middle ground between causal connection and mere chance, and if a principle of synchronicity is to be
invoked, it has to be in the context of a different world view, one
provided for Jung by his theory of the collective unconscious. But
when Jung shifted to what he believed to be an older and more
mature wisdom, he failed to understand 'that he was not so much
getting rid of causality as shifting it to a different locus'.[31] Beloff
himself then gives a broad definition of causality, which would
allow to be included within it something akin to Aristotle's final
cause, and which would certainly suggest that synchronicity, if it
is to be taken seriously, is a *causal* principle of a kind. In Beloff's
account the crucial question is whether, 'A was necessary for the

occurrence of B . . . regardless of the temporal, spatial, material or energetic relationships that may hold as between these events.'[32]

I think it is clear that if we use the word 'cause' in the broad way suggested by Beloff, and if we also have the kind of world-view espoused by Jung, then there would be nothing irrational in the suggestion that God caused events in the universe by acts of will, without disrupting the orderly running of nature in a way that would demonstrate to the onlooker that a spiritual agent must be at work. Thus, we have here another possibility for the location of divine activity, but not an explanation of the mechanism. Indeed, the world view considered in this sub-section would challenge most strongly the assumptions that lay behind the demand for a 'mechanism'. Also, my own use of the word 'location' is somewhat misleading, for in a view such as Jung's there is no 'place' where God is active; it is, rather, that thought and will are identified as being relevant, or in Beloff's sense, causal, in the production of effects.

It is worth pointing out that if one favours this approach to the nature of providence, then there is added reason for wanting to redescribe the sovereignty of God, and to take seriously the Whiteheadian idea of government by persuasion. In a semi-autonomous natural order it seems implausible to say that an act of will is always effective, but plausible, within Jung's overall view, to say that it exerts an influence, or that, in the long run it is decisive, like the influence of general providence when it is likened to tidal pressure.

(*d*) *Some other views*. The three views just discussed are only samples from a vast literature concerned with speculation on the relationship of God to the universe, but they are, I think, representative of the three kinds of approach that one is likely to find. The first approach is concerned to find a place for God to act within the physical universe, the second approach does not seek to find this, but sees God as active in another order, that of selves or persons. The third approach calls in question our whole set of assumptions about causality, so that the attempt to find any gap or special area where God can operate is regarded as a mistaken enterprise. Even though Pollard, and some existentialists, would question the picture we tend to have of the physical world, they see it as a system that is in some way 'bounded' or complete, even if there is room for the unpredictable. The third approach calls for a much more radical reassessment of our concept of nature.

Further examples of the first approach are provided by those who believe that the details of the evolutionary process demand divine activity in order to explain them, and some of these will be mentioned in section five. Another example of the second approach is Karl Heim, and his view of reality having different 'dimensions' or 'spaces'.[33] Buber's distinction between the realms of 'I-Thou' and 'I-it' has similar implications.[34] However, some of the variations on the third approach are probably the most significant for the understanding of the concept of providence.

Whitehead's philosophy clearly comes under the general heading of the third approach, which is not to say that he would have been happy about everything in Jung's essay. Change, according to Whitehead, needs three factors. There is the lawlike, causal activity with which we are familiar in scientific experiments; there is the capacity for self-creativity or spontaneity which he sees as present during the occurrence of every event; and there is the influence of God. God is the ground of novelty, for he places special value on some of the potentialities that are open to the universe, and to this valuation things can respond. In this way God draws or persuades the world without determining it.[35]

It is impossible to do justice to Whitehead's theory in a short summary, and it must be stressed that his account of change has to be seen in the context of a complete and complex metaphysical system. This system contrasts sharply with that of the Christian existentialists; for instead of dividing the material and the personal, Whitehead sees these orders as part of a great unity in which everything is related to every other thing, or, as he would prefer to put it, every event is linked with every other event. This unity has to be seen after the analogy of an organic whole in which 'process' is a feature of every part, even, as we have seen, of God. Hence he calls his theory 'a philosophy of organism'.

Whitehead has many followers, and one who deserves special mention is Hartshorne. Hartshorne is of particular interest with respect to the third issue discussed in the introduction, and is insistent that some kind of change must be ascribed to God, if God is to be personal in a significant sense. He argues, 'All our experience supports the view that the cognitive relation, and still more obviously, if possible, a relation of love, is genuinely constitutive of the knower or the lover, rather than of the known or the loved.' He goes on to claim that, 'the purely absolute God was, by logical implication, conceived as a thing, not a subject or a person.'[36] This argument is backed up by the claim that theologians tend to misunderstand the idea of 'perfection', which need not be incompatible with the idea of God as changing.[37] One writer has summarized Hartshorne's views as involving the position that 'God is *changing* in the content of his experience but *eternal* in his character and purpose'.[38]

4. God as the creative artist

From the discussion in Chapter III, and from the last section, it is evident how I suggest that the question 'What is the mechanism of divine action?' should be dealt with. First, I am in favour of being agnostic about the methods by which God acts, assuming that he does so. Second, I am wary of the request for an account of the 'mechanism' of his action, since this may suggest that whatever the manner may be, it must be akin to the way in which one part of a machine works on another part.

This is the negative part of the response to the question; but there is also a more positive part to the response that can be given, and this gives human reason another sort of handle for attempting to evaluate what it means to speak of providential action in nature. The positive response includes the exploration of suitable analogies, of which I shall say more anon, and it includes the attempt to show that the universe is of such a kind that God's action is not ruled out. This theme was especially evident in Pollard, and it is reminiscent of Kant's argument when he insists that, although the speculative reason cannot prove the existence of God, yet it can show that God is possible; for if it could not, it would be irrational to believe in God, and any moral argument of the kind that Kant upholds would be in vain. God's existence cannot be proved, but it cannot be disproved.[39] All three of the approaches just discussed are relevant here, for each tries to show that God's action is possible.

The Christian doctrine of providence not only requires that God's action be possible in this general way, it also requires that there be several theoretical possibilities open to God. This point can be argued as follows. For the traditional account of providence to be maintained, it must be the case that God's action can make a difference to the world. At the same time, when we are speaking of providential action rather than of miracle, the action must be such that, after the event, a natural explanation is possible. For both of these things to be true it must be the case that there be several possibilities within the natural order at any one time, or at least on a large number of occasions. God's action is the steering along one of these possible routes, rather as the helmsman on a river-boat steers his craft on its precise route, but not of course just anywhere, since he has to keep to the river.

An important consequence of this is that God cannot, by providential action, do everything. According to the mainstream tradition some things he cannot do absolutely, namely those things that are contrary to his nature. Grotius is a good example of an outspoken advocate of this position. Just as God 'cannot cause that two times two should not make four, so he cannot cause that that which is intrinsically evil be not evil.'[40] (Those who support Grotius' position tend to include among the logical absurdities that God cannot perpetrate the creation of men who are both truly free and morally perfect by necessity.) Some other things can be done by God, but only through miracle, such as the instantaneous turning of water into wine. Therefore, within the context of strictly providential action God is doubly limited; for although there must be several possibilities open to God, as I have shown, and in some creative situations there might be an infinite number of these, at the same time there will be many outcomes that are *not* possibilities. If God wants to achieve any of these (provided they are not contrary to his nature) he has to use miracle, not providential action, and such a use of miracle would be rather like the helmsman hauling his boat overland. This may well be possible, but it is not possible in his capacity as helmsman.

This limitation on the range of providential action prompts me to stress the autonomy of the natural order even more strongly than does Aquinas. (Here there is of necessity some overlap with the next chapter, and the question of the determination of human actions.) Having defended the importance of secondary causality, Aquinas goes on to defend predestination;[41] and relying on God's position outside space and time, he tries to combine the relative autonomy of nature and of man with the claim that God is nevertheless somehow in control of every event. I suggest that the contemporary Christian who wishes to hold a coherent philosophy that is rooted in the mainstream tradition should describe the situation differently and avoid all talk of predestination, which, although it can be given a plausible interpretation,[42] tends to conjure up all sorts of ideas that are inconsistent with the freedom of man and with the autonomy of nature. In particular I recommend that he avoids saying 'It's God's will', when some terrible event occurs, such as the accidental death of a child, since even though there is a sense in which this might be said to have been permitted by God, along the lines of the scholastics' 'permissive will' of God, this totally misleads the ordinary person. The terminology still suggests that in some way God either desired or co-operated in the event, whereas within the Christian philosophy that I am suggesting, he did neither. Clarity would be much better served by insisting that many things happen that are not God's will, whether it be moral fault, which results from the autonomy of man, or calamity, which results from the autonomy of nature. Moreover, within the context of providential action, there are many cases where not only does God not will an event but he could not have prevented it, since the range of possible action within nature did not include such prevention. Calamities due to physical happenings rather than moral fault could always be prevented, in theory, by miracle, but there are strong grounds for thinking that the regular use of miracle in order to avoid such calamities would endanger the kind of autonomy that the natural order must have if it is to be the context for responsible action. I shall return to this theme in Chapter V.

This emphasis on the necessary limitations to providential action leads me back to Sherlock's account of God as the creative artist, for although I have found occasion to criticize Sherlock, in this analogy he is employing a fruitful image.[43] One of the interesting things about creative art is the way in which the very limitations of the medium can in themselves become the possible source of a creative response. Thus Gothic architecture is, in large part, a response to the discipline of working in stone, whereas part of the problem for contemporary architecture is the availability of 'plastic' materials, like steel, that are in a way over-generous. There is a comparable situation in music, where the composer or performer creates within the limitations of the instruments. Even in human relationships the imposition of limitations, as in marriage or community life, can be the context for a new kind of creative response, and one that would not otherwise have been possible.

By analogy, the concept of providence is concerned with God as a creative artist, whose medium, the created order, has certain built-in limitations with regard to what can be done with it. Further, it might be the case that any alternative creative order, that could be the context for human life, would have to have equivalent limitations built into it, if it were to be an 'order'. These limitations are the source of Aquinas' 'secondary laws' or of Sherlock's 'natural powers'. But within these limitations there is room for creative activity. Just as in the case of a human painter we cannot predict what the finished canvas will be like, but, if we know the painter, we can predict what kind of paint he will use, and that the painting will show a certain style, so we cannot predict what providence will do in the universe in any detail, but we can predict that God will generally use natural forces for his government of the world, and that what he brings forth will be good.

This analogy helps to bring out some of the meaning of the idea of 'steering' nature. The term is not meant to indicate how God initiates change, but it suggests that he does so by using the creative possibilities that are open in a way that is analogous to the use of opportunities by the human artist. Moreover, the situation in which providence can be active may be contrasted with other theoretically possible situations: on the one hand a world where all events were absolutely necessary, and on the other a world in which there were regular breakdowns in the orderly processes of nature.

This claim that the concept of providence demands a view of nature in which there is a certain openness, and therefore that providence works like a creative artist, within the context of limitations but not of necessity, allows for the theoretical falsification of the claim that there is a providence. It follows from the analysis offered that no scientific advance could *verify* a providential interpretation of events, for the strictly empirical findings could never demand this rather than some other interpretation. Also, as we have seen, providence could not be a scientific hypothesis by means of which one could make detailed predictions with regard to any future observations. Nevertheless, a scientific falsification is a theoretical possibility, since any providential interpretation has as a precondition for its validity an account of the natural order that is not totally determined and predictable. Contemporary science does not demand such an order, but it is logically possible that a science of the future might reverse the present trend and produce overwhelming evidence for a totally determined system. The believer in providence naturally believes that this will not happen, but this is a belief, not a special sort of knowledge, so that in principle falsification is possible, or, failing that, very strong counter-evidence. If the natural order's predictability were found not to include the actions of persons, then a limited account of providence, along the lines of Bultmann's view, would be the only possibility.

Before we pass to the next section, there are two further comments called for. First, the description of the helmsman steering his craft within the confines of the river, and the picture of the artist working within the limitations of his medium, both help to fill out the notion of God 'steering' nature, and they succeed in contrasting providential action with the ordinary running of nature, and with miracle. They are particularly apt for the consideration of special providence, with its individual decisions, especially if we think in terms of Wesley's distinction between the general providence at work in inanimate and animal nature, and the particular providence at work in man. However, the pictures can be stretched to cover also the distinction between the two kinds of providence. We can liken general providence to the portrait artist painting in the background, almost absent-mindedly working in accordance with his general character and purpose. In contrast, when he paints the face of the subject he applies a different kind of care and attention to each brush stroke. If the natural order exists primarily for the sake of man, this contrast may be quite appropriate.

Second, the specific suggestions as to the mode or location of divine activity made in section three can be likened to a kind of theological fiction that has a similar relationship to the scriptures that science fiction has to straight science. This does not make them worthless. Thus science fiction has a special role, for at its best it can be stimulating and even prophetic, but it is not science. Similarly suggestions as to the mode or location of divine activity can be stimulating and suggestive, but given the nature of God, if he is a reality of the kind claimed in the theistic tradition, then at least on this plane of existence we can never *know* if the suggestions are correct. The scriptures, on the other hand, are attempts to describe what are believed within the tradition to be actual experiences of God.

5. The problem of evolution

So much has been written about the implications of evolutionary theory for religious beliefs that a separate section for some of these issues is in order.

The first issue to be clarified concerns the nature of purposive or teleological explanations in biology in general, and evolution in particular. Although there is still some dispute on this matter, the general view among biologists is that such explanations cannot be eliminated, for in one way or another they are tied up with the notions of the 'function' of an organism, or the 'goal-directedness' of much behaviour. F. J. Ayala, for example, summarizes one of his papers in the journal, *Philosophy of Science*, by writing, 'It is argued that teleological explanations in biology are not only acceptable but indeed indispensable.'[44] What is needed is a careful analysis of the meaning and implication of terms such as 'purpose', and this has been provided in a number of recent books.[45] One of the things that is clear from such analyses is that one must not confuse what some people call 'internal teleology', which refers, for example, to the way in which the heart or liver can be said to have a certain purpose with respect to the survival and well-being of an animal, and 'external teleology', which refers to a purpose that is deliberately planned, as in the case of a tool. Thus the fact, assuming that it is a fact, that teleological language is inescapable within biology leaves quite open the question as to whether evolution as a whole can be said to have (an external) purpose. Similarly, A. Woodfield argues that the universe as a whole 'cannot possibly have a purpose in the sense of "natural function within a wider system", since there is no wider system.' It could, in principle, have an 'artificial function', if it were designed by God, as a man designs a tool, but Woodfield sees no reason for thinking this to be the case.[46]

It should be clear from the above that there can be no easy jump from the purposes manifested in parts of nature to the purpose of nature as a whole. Nevertheless, there have been many attempts to show that evolution still demands a teleological explanation that goes beyond what is currently offered in neo-Darwinian theory, and some of these attempts claim that Paley's designer is the only possible candidate for this overall explanation. These attempts can be divided into two kinds; the first argues that some of the actual steps within the evolutionary process demand an explanation that goes beyond natural selection and adaptation, the second argues, not in terms of particular omissions or gaps, but in terms of the proper interpretation of the process taken as a whole.

We can take Charles Raven as a representative of the first approach. In his Gifford lectures he argues that theories of evolution based on 'gene change' are simply insufficient, given the time span involved, and he supports this claim by the argument that the perfection of certain natural processes, especially those involving a series of related and complementary moves, cannot be accounted for without a designer. His examples include the weaving of the spider's web, and the sequences by which the cuckoo ensures its survival as a species. Overall, Raven is convinced that indications of this kind show that 'the things that are made' do manifest their maker.[47] Others, supporting a position similar to that of Raven, object to the suggestion that evolution can ultimately be explained in terms of 'chance', which they see as implicit in current biological theory. Thus the French scientist, Lecompte du Nouy, claimed to have shown fantastic odds against the chance emergence of life in the universe,[48] and E. E. Harris wrote, 'The facts do not permit us to hold that the high degree of improbability generated by natural selection could have been the result of mere random shuffling and accidental change.'[49]

Views such as these have a certain initial plausibility, especially if we stress the emergence of complex biological *systems* within an organism, which often demand the co-operative working of many sub-systems. One could also point to the apparent examples of pre-adaptation, such as the emergence, especially in man, of capacities like that for abstract mathematics, which do not have any obvious survival value during the main run of evolutionary development. Nevertheless, claims such as Raven's are basically scientific claims, and in general they have not proved acceptable to the scientific community. It is not that this community claims to know all the answers, but many of the gaps in the understanding of the evolutionary process that apologists in the school of Paley used to rely on have been filled in, and there are at least plausible suggestions for many of the others. Again, I am not claiming that the scientific 'community' is an absolute authority, whose verdict must be accepted without question. But that is not the point. The crucial point is that, given the research procedures which the scientific community is using, we cannot say *a priori* that the remaining gaps in evolutionary theory cannot be filled by purely scientific explanations of the future. Therefore, we cannot say that the details of evolution *demand* an external designer.

With regard to the rejection of chance as the whole source of evolution, I think that there is certainly some force in this objection, but it is very hard to evaluate, partly because many biologists do not want to describe the processes involved, such as that of natural selection, as being mere 'chance',[50] and partly because it is notoriously difficult to say what the odds against an event are *after* that event has in fact occurred.

A proper evaluation of the disputes involved here would necessitate an extremely technical discussion, and I propose instead to recommend the following attitude to the adequacy of current theory to account for the evolutionary process. It may eventually transpire that the detailed mechanics of evolution require a far more complex theory than that at present envisaged, and it *might* turn out that a factor akin to Aristotle's final cause had to be taken seriously again; but this could still be within an essentially secular account of nature, and would not support the claim that an external designer was manifested in the detailed operation of evolution in a way that forced itself on the scientific understanding. Thus providence, as I have described it, would still not be demonstrated by aspects of evolution, though evolution would be compatible with the operation of providence, and many would find it suggestive of it. Moreover, the account that I have given of providence does not require that God be manifest directly within the evolutionary process; for God, I have argued, works more typically by providence than by miracle, and it is part of the very nature of providence that it operates in such a way that a naturalistic explanation can always be given.

The second approach that I have referred to does not rely on any alleged gaps, but on the proper interpretation of the whole process. I have much sympathy with this approach, and it is, I suspect, closer to the spirit of Paul's claim that 'the things that are made' manifest their maker; but it must be emphasized that the claim here is a metaphysical one rather than a purely scientific one. As in the traditional arguments for the existence of God, we are being asked to account for a *whole* system. The biologist L. J. Henderson provides an example of this approach, for he supported mechanistic explanations of the detailed operation of evolution but was impressed by the direction towards greater consciousness and complexity, and by the overall capacity of the natural order for this direction.[51] More recently the zoologist C. F. A. Pantin has approved of Henderson's approach; and after claiming that we can conceive of very different universes, he stresses a series of extraordinary features of this universe that make it a possible and suitable environment for life. This, he claims, is not proof of a designer, although a designer is possible; but he wants to join Henderson in the claim that 'in our present state of knowledge both organism and environment show an abundance of unique necessary properties for life; and that Natural Selection alone does not account for these.'[52] Here, unlike Raven, Pantin is not relying on the problems faced in accounting for any specific phenomenon, but the problems in accounting for the entire process. Another exponent of an approach along these lines was F. R. Tennant.[53]

One's estimation of arguments of this second kind will depend especially on two things. First, one's general attitude to metaphysical arguments; second, one's moral philosophy. The claim that there has so far been a certain direction in evolution towards greater complexity is a factual claim; but as soon as there is the suggestion that there is 'progress', or that one species is intrinsically 'higher' than another, one is making value judgments and not scientific judgments. I should be prepared to support some of these judgments, but not as part of a claim that evolution provided empirical evidence for the existence of providential activity.

The conclusion that follows from this discussion is very much in line with the position defended in the introduction with regard to the question of whether the claim that providence is at work is in any sense an empirical claim. Providential interpretations of evolution are not empirically given, but they are compatible with evolution. Some people will find them suggested by evolution; but their basis is either a metaphysical one, established by metaphysical rather than scientific arguments, or an experiential one, related to individual experiences and our interpretation of them.

V

Providence and Human Nature

1. Man and the physical order

The fact that man is to be considered in a separate chapter already indicates that I have taken up a certain position, and accepted something akin to Dobzhansky's 'levels' of existence.[1] This issue of levels arises even within what I have called 'the order of nature', for there is a lively debate as to whether there is the theoretical possibility of reducing all biological explanations to mechanistic ones, in terms of physics and chemistry. Philosophers of science are divided on this issue, and some, such as C. G. Hempel, regard it as one that eventually will have to be decided on empirical grounds when more evidence is available.[2] There is, of course, a sense in which biological organisms have a physics and chemistry, and are made up of physical matter, but the claim of many is that the kind of complexity involved produces what can be called a new 'level' of existence, which necessitates new kinds of description and new categories of language. The account of providence that I have provided in Chapter IV would fit more happily into a theory of biology that was not reducible to physics and chemistry, but this would not be an absolute precondition for a coherent account of providence in the natural order, provided that physics and chemistry themselves allowed for the kind of openness that I have argued to be a precondition for meaningful providential interpretations.

The position that I wish to defend not only suggests that there is an irreducibility of biology to physics and chemistry, but much more insistently, claims that there is also an irreducibility of descriptions of human action either to purely biological or to purely behaviouristic descriptions. The basis for such a claim need not be a metaphysical assumption about the ontological status of man, but a claim about the incapacity of biological or behaviouristic reductions to give an adequate account of the complexities of human action and human experience, especially as these are manifested in our language.

With behaviourism in particular, it is necessary to state the nature of my opposition with care, since this is a term that is used in different ways, and many research psychologists who call themselves 'behaviourists' would certainly not subscribe to all the opinions of J. B. Watson. When 'behaviourism' refers to an area of interest or an approach to research, there is no conflict with the position that I am advocating. The trouble comes when a concentration on the methodology of behaviourism spills over into certain philosophical assumptions about what can be considered as 'real', and unfortunately it is often not realized that when this happens *philosophical assumptions*, which need justifying, have been made. The influential psychologist, B. F. Skinner, has the merit of spelling out some of these assumptions. Thus he argues that, 'If we are to use the methods of science in the field of human affairs, we must assume that behaviour is lawful and determined.'[3] Later, after discussing the importance of the indeterminacy principle in physics, he makes it clear that he does not want to claim that all aspects of every human individual will necessarily become predictable; but this is not because man is free, it is only that, as with the parallel case of physics, 'it may be beyond the range of a predictive or controlling science' to cover such details.[4] Later on still, he proceeds to claim that we assign actions to an originating agent within the organism only when external variables are unnoticed or ignored, and he then defines the 'self' as simply 'a device for representing *a functionally unified system of responses*'.[5]

My criticism of this position is along the same lines as my criticism of Ryle's position in *The Concept of Mind*,[6] and I have already indicated my general agreement with H. D. Lewis's objections to such views.[7] Since I am concerned with the meaning of providence rather than with its justification (until I come to Chapter VII), it would be beyond my purpose to give a comprehensive argument against Skinner's position, but I shall indicate the two types of objection that I should wish to pursue. First, Skinner's position requires a drastic reduction of all internal states, such as being pained, trying to remember a name, internal moral struggles, and so on. Iris Murdoch has given a powerful account of how some of these internal affairs may have no exterior and visible manifestations.[8] Second, Skinner's position requires a drastic reinterpretation of moral notions like responsibility and virtue and his position cannot, in my view, form the basis of an adequate moral philosophy.

Be this as it may, we have here the theoretical possibility of the falsification of the claim that there is such a thing as providence, or at least the possibility of very strong counter-evidence against it, parallel to the possible falsification of providence in the natural order as discussed in the last chapter. Although there are strong grounds for rejecting Skinner's position, I do not think that his assumptions can at this stage be rigorously disproved, and in principle the human sciences of the future might increasingly confirm the position he defends. Once again, there is no possibility of a strictly empirical verification of a providential interpretation, but there is the theoretical possibility of falsification, or of strong counter-evidence. Providence, whether in the natural order or in the human order, is not compatible with just any state of affairs whatsoever.

2. *The government of 'moral causes'*

The central problem to be faced in this chapter concerns the sense in which there can be meaningful government of free beings, or of what Sherlock calls 'moral causes' in contrast with 'natural causes'. There are a number of philosophers who would dissolve this problem by denying that any coherent meaning can be attached to human freedom; and there have been theologians who have also denied human freedom, but on the very different grounds that God's omnipotence, or the fall of man, made freedom impossible. However, instead of being side-tracked into a lengthy debate on the free-will issue, I shall merely reaffirm that I am attempting to analyse the concept of providence from within a certain tradition, and there can be no doubt as to the continuing emphasis on the existence and importance of freedom within this tradition as a whole.

To begin the discussion of providence in relation to human freedom I shall return to the position of Sherlock, and then try to contrast his solution to the difficulties with one that I claim to be more adequate.

Sherlock's solution, as we have seen, was to insist that God was in total control over the external actions of men. This he could achieve either by playing on their passions directly, for 'how easy it is for God to imprint such thoughts upon men's minds with an irresistible vigour and brightness' that they will not be able to resist,[9] or 'by a concurrence of external causes' to provoke similarly irresistible passions.[10] By such methods God treats us as 'instruments of providence', not as 'reasonable creatures'. When he treats us as the latter, then his government consists of (1) giving us laws so that we may know the difference between good and evil, (2) annexing rewards and punishments to these laws in order to invite obedience, and (3) granting the assistance of grace.[11] Over all, Sherlock makes a significant contrast between 'the government of providence' and 'the government of grace', for the former is coercive while the latter uses no more force than is consistent with 'the freedom of choice, and the nature of virtue and vice'.[12]

I have already indicated my opposition to this point of view. There seems little point to this treatment of us as 'reasonable creatures' if no external action contrary to the divine will is ever to be permitted. Again, providence does not have to mean universal providence; and if it did, then I do not think that we could have a possible context for what we regard as distinctively human life. Instead of making this approach, Christians need to describe very differently the way in which God is in control of nature, man, and history. This may seem to some to be an abandonment of the very tradition within which I am claiming to conduct an analysis; but what I am seeking is not an abandonment, but a rationalization of the tradition, whereby the doctrine of providence is stated in such a way that its full implications are seen, and this involves a reappraisal of the ideas of the omnipotence and the sovereignty of God. Providence is implicit in the whole tradition, especially within the scriptures. The sovereignty of God is also implicit, but the interpretation of sovereignty to be the sort of omnipotence that Sherlock and many other theologians advocate is not, as I shall try to show, demanded by the scriptures. To put this another way. As the intelligent Christian tries to state his philosophy in the twentieth century, anything recognizable as a continuance of the tradition demands a personal God, and a personal God is inseparably linked with belief in special providence. However, an adequate account of providence demands a reappraisal of what Christians mean by the sovereignty of God, and although this does involve some break with tradition, it is in no way on a par with abandoning belief in a personal God.

In the case of the purely natural order it is possible to consider providence as governing by coercion, though I think that such a description is misleading even here, since what is coerced is not the details of every event, but the general pattern that emerges. In the case of the human order, providential government must be *generally* by persuasion, not coercion, unless we are to adopt Sherlock's desperate expedient of allowing the effects of human freedom to change only man's private and inner world. This, as I have already argued, is incompatible with significant responsibility, and presents a totally unrealistic picture of the world we live in.

I stressed the word 'generally' in the above statement, since it is not incompatible with the idea of providential guidance of an order of free beings to claim that God sometimes compels a certain state of affairs to come about, provided that this compulsion is not held to produce virtue by itself. (Sherlock was at least right here.[13]) This would be like the occurrence of miracle; for if God continuously or generally used miracles, he would destroy the autonomy of the order of nature. However, I do not think that we should use this theoretical possibility of the occasional use of divine coercion in order to explain difficult biblical passages. I much prefer explanations that are congruous with our contemporary experience, for we then have some yardstick for estimating our interpretations of scripture.

I can illustrate my argument here by a discussion of the case of Judas Iscariot. Here, on many earlier accounts, we have the case of a man who was destined to betray Jesus. Moreover, this betrayal was part of the divine plan, for God intended to bring good out of evil with the death of Jesus, and Judas' betrayal played a key role in bringing about the death of Jesus. Over against this approach I would suggest an account of Judas' betrayal along the following lines, an account that is consistent with the kind of providential government that is acceptable for modern man. Given the nature of Jesus, it was certain, humanly speaking, that someone would eventually betray him. (This prediction is rather like that of Plato when he prophesied that a perfect man would eventually be killed.[14]) As Jesus' ministry continued, it gradually became evident, at least to someone with sensitive insight into human character, that Judas would be the betrayer. But even at the end it was not logically certain that Judas would betray Jesus;

it was rather a matter of the very high probability which in human affairs we often call certainty, in contrast to the merely probable. An account of this kind, I suggest, makes sense of the biblical tradition, and takes it seriously, but at the same time it reinterprets any hint of fatalism which may have been acceptable to a writer of the first century, but is not so now. Interestingly, it is only in John's gospel that Jesus is said to have known 'from the beginning' who was to betray him;[15] and my account entails either that the author was mistaken, or that Jesus' knowledge was of the kind I have referred to as human certainty, not infallible knowledge.

This is obviously a highly controversial subject; but I would argue for a similar account of other biblical passages where human action is said to be governed by God, as for example the hardening of Pharoah's heart. This was the occasion for another act that brought good out of evil, and was therefore assumed to have been 'staged' by God. Primitive people, as I have stressed, tended to see events as 'overdetermined', and especially in the earlier strata of writings they felt that, even though man was responsible, God had also to be the author of all that happened. However, we can preserve the essential core in the traditional concept of providence, by which God 'steers' the outcome of physical or human events, and present it in a way that is coherent and plausible in the contemporary setting.

My position can be further supported if it is held that there is some analogy between political government and divine government. In primitive times political government has often been in the context of massive coercion, but as civilizations mature, government by consent becomes more and more acceptable. Congruously I am suggesting that the view that divine government must be all-pervasive, if it is to be meaningful, is a view that the mature Christian should grow out of. The primitive view in fact belittles the splendour of the human order that is made by God to have the potentiality of creativity and responsibility.

Not only does the foregoing argument suggest that a reinterpretation of God's omnipotence is called for; there is equal need for a reinterpretation of his omniscience. As we have seen, the mainstream tradition has asserted that although God does not *fore*know all human actions, he nevertheless 'knows' them from his eternal standpoint. Aquinas, for example, likens God's knowledge of future contingents to one who looks down on a road from a height, and 'sees all together those who are passing along the road', in contrast with the human traveller who sees only what is in front of him.[16] This view goes back not only to Aquinas, but to many earlier writers, notably Boethius, who was of great influence from the sixth century. Boethius's widely read *Consolations of Philosophy* contain an eloquent plea for the omnipotence and omniscience of God, based on the eternal nature of his being. But Boethius insists that although we can use the Latin word *providentia* to refer to God's knowledge of the future, we should not use the word *praevidentia*, lest we confuse God's knowledge with human knowledge of what is to come. Also, he prefers the word *praesentia* to *praescientia*, to stress God's eternal standpoint.[17]

It is certainly the case that an adequate Christian philosophy must insist that God cannot foreknow, or predict, every voluntary human action, any more than it can hold that an infinite computer (if such a thing were possible), given all possible information about the present state of affairs, could predict the outcome of all human decisions. But why is it necessary for this philosophy to add that nevertheless God 'knows' absolutely everything from his eternal standpoint? Why not simply be agnostic about this, neither asserting it nor denying it? As creator, it is evident that a Christian God must in some sense transcend the category of time as we know it; for example, he can have no beginning. However, this is such a baffling thing to be forced to say, that any claim to know what such a transcendent state involves, as, for example, the implications of this transcendence for God's knowledge of future contingents, seems presumptuous. (For example, could God tell a prophet today what he knows will happen tomorrow, without being said to *fore*see?) We cannot know that he 'knows'; we can only know that if the Christian God is a reality, his relationship to time must be different from ours. More than this we cannot know, and there is no need for the religious man to say more. A Christian philosophy should claim, more modestly, that God is all-knowing in the sense that he knows all that is possible to know (which may not be literally everything), just as he is all-powerful in the sense that, given his nature, he can do whatever it is possible to do (which is certainly not everything).

3. Providence and grace

At this point we need to explore the relationship of the concepts of providence and of grace, for Sherlock's position suggests that when we are talking of the persuasion of humans we are not really referring to providence at all, at least not in its strict sense. Since the grammar of providence must be related to similar concepts, I must devote some space to an analysis of the concept of grace.

The Christian concept of grace has affiliations with pre-Christian ideas. Thus the Hastings *Encyclopaedia of Religion and Ethics*, in its article on 'Grace', refers to 'the widespread feeling that the gods are kindred and friendly beings, guardians of morality, and, up to a certain point, able to help men'. This broad conception of grace as the friendly help of the divine realm has an impersonal counterpart in Plato, as we have seen. In the New Testament the word for grace is *charis*, and its meaning owes something to this general conception of divine help, and also something to the normal classical use of *charis* as that which gives pleasure. It is actually used in this way in Luke.[18] However, there is a characteristic use of the term in the New Testament which is more specific, and which refers to God's love, and especially the redeeming love held to have been demonstrated and exemplified in Jesus. This special use undoubtedly owes much to a certain strain in the Old Testament, notably in the notion of *hesed*, or 'loving-kindness', which is particularly prominent in the message of the prophet Hosea, and which occurs in a number of passages where the emphasis is on God's faithfulness and forbearance.[19] It also owes much, it seems certain, to the particular teaching and personality of Jesus of Nazareth. Even the more sceptical students of the New Testament tend to accept the claim that people remembered the stories that Jesus told, and the parables of the good Samaritan and of the prodigal son are brief and brilliant expositions of this concept of grace. However, the most familiar uses of the word itself come in Paul. Paul had worked out a doctrine of salvation based on a universal condition of human sin[20] and a loving God who acted in Jesus in order to make salvation a possibility for all. 'God shows his love for us in that while we were yet sinners Christ died for us.'[21] In this context, grace is, for Paul especially, 'the grace of Christ', which is itself a frequent phrase in his greetings. It is the unmerited gift of God, the work of his loving-kindness, and that by which we are justified. Strictly speaking, Paul's doctrine is not 'justification by faith', despite the common use of this phrase in the Protestant tradition, but 'justification by grace'.[22] It is expressed more fully in the affirmation, 'by grace you are saved through faith'.[23]

From this biblical background the concept of grace passed into the history of the Christian tradition, where it soon became embroiled in a series of controversies over questions such as 'Is grace irresistible?', 'What kinds of grace are there?', and 'What are the channels by which we receive grace?'[24] I shall avoid involvement in these issues as much as possible and concentrate on the relationship of the New Testament concept of grace to providence.

In the light of our analysis I do not think that it is satisfactory to contrast providence with grace in terms of the coercive versus the non-coercive. On the one side, it is not essential for providence to be coercive, in the strong sense of the word 'compelled', in order to indicate a positive form of government. Positive government, in the political sense, must perhaps include 'coercive' laws, but these do not literally compel subjects, except in unusual circumstances; rather they apply a certain pressure. Similarly, divine government, either of matter or of men, must at least apply something analogous to a general pressure, as explored in the analogy of the tide; but it is not required that there be coercion in the sense of absolute compulsion. On this matter Aquinas may be quoted: 'God's providence lays necessity on some things, but not, as some have believed, on all', for the completeness of the universe would not be achieved 'unless every shade of reality were found among its components'.[25]

On the other side, while there is much to be said for the view that grace is generally persuasive rather than coercive, and Paul would seem to endorse this when he exhorts his readers not to receive the grace of God in vain,[26] there is no logical reason why grace, in the sense of the unmerited gift of God, should not sometimes be irresistible. Such grace would not make people morally better, at least within a view of morality that I would support; but there are other things, such as an infusion of knowledge, which could be the work of irresistible grace. I am not in fact myself in favour of a doctrine of irresistible grace; but this is not on logical grounds, in terms of how the New Testament concept could be applied, but on experiential grounds, in terms of what is suggested in Christian experience.

How, then, should the concepts of providence and of grace be distinguished? I suggest that the concepts overlap, but that a distinction can be made along the following lines. Providence considers God from the point of view of the being who is the ultimate source of all change. Grace considers the same God from the point of view of the one whose loving-kindness seeks to redeem and sanctify the created order. Thus, considered as part of the divine activity, all acts of grace are part of God's providence, for they are part of the means by which God guides and governs;

on the other hand, it would be misleading to describe all acts of providence as acts of grace, since many of them do not directly indicate loving-kindness or unmerited gift.

This may suggest that grace is simply that part of providence that relates to the human order, but the situation is a little more complex than this. Traditionally, many Christians have distinguished an 'order of nature' with respect to man, in which he can achieve a certain natural happiness, from an 'order of grace', in which he discovers that he has a destiny which transcends the kind of existence men normally experience, and which he can begin to enjoy now, but only with special assistance from God. Grace therefore is not used to refer to every one of God's dealings with the human species, even when they reflect loving-kindness, but it refers more especially to those acts that draw men to this higher possibility, a possibility that nature by itself cannot supply. Hence the Thomist tradition claimed that grace did not destroy nature, but fulfilled or supplemented it.

Thus in a broad sense grace can refer to any providential act that reflects the loving-kindness of God, but in a stricter sense it is linked with certain particular acts that are held by Christians to open up a new kind of living which they describe as being 'in Christ'.

4. The changing of man

In order to understand the nature of providential action as it can apply to man, we need to be sensitive to the difficult problem of what change really involves in the case of rational and moral agents. In ordinary language, which often provides a clue to the complexities of an issue, we distinguish bodily change from a deeper, interior change. We might say 'He is a changed man' when there is no change in physical appearance or health. But of course bodily change, and what I shall call 'personal change', are not unrelated. Not only does personal change usually involve change in behaviour, but bodily change will often occasion personal change, for example during puberty, or following a disfigurement. Some would say that the physical change is the cause of the personal change, but I would argue that it cannot be the whole cause, if we are to hold a doctrine of real freedom, but rather an influence and an occasion for change.

In this account of personal change I am not advocating a complete dualism in which the person inhabits his body, but I am returning to the claim that there is a personal dimension to the individual man or woman which cannot be described purely in physical terms, and that it is to this dimension that we must refer moral or spiritual change; and furthermore that such change can occur only when there is a voluntary component on the part of the person. Thus bodily change can trigger personal change, but not simply produce it.

When we try to analyse this personal dimension, there are several essential elements that can be separated out. My analysis here will certainly be considered controversial, but tentatively I would recommend the following elements. First, and hardest of all to characterize, is the self-conscious centre, or subject, which cannot be treated as a 'thing' with spatial coordinates, nor observed even by an act of introspection, but which we are simply aware of during all our conscious states. Second, there are the essential dispositions, the acquired virtues and vices of classical philosophy, which characterize the typical actions of this subject. Third, and closely associated with the second element, are some of the basic drives (the equivalent of the winged horses in Plato's famous description of the soul as a charioteer and a pair of horses[27]). These are particularly difficult to dissociate from the physical dimension, and in most cases I should not attempt to do so. Some of the passions might better be regarded as part of the (internal) environment in the context of which the person has to live, rather than as an essential part of that person. Some drives, however, such as the search for God, and love of one's neighbour, seem also to be inseparably linked with the personal dimension. The fact that Plato had both a light and a dark horse is symptomatic of the difficulty of giving an adequate account of these driving forces, but unlike Plato I am not committed to the view that what I call the personal dimension can exist without a physical dimension. Fourth, there is the rational element (Plato's charioteer), often only dimly recognizable, including the capacity to choose to act or not to act in accordance with a certain principle. Fifth, there is a certain style which marks all the activities of the person, and especially its creative ones. This is not a moral virtue, but a sort of primitive and inescapable endowment. Some people would add a core of memory as a sixth element, but I am inclined not to do so.[28] I shall, however, add a sixth element shortly.

The foregoing is speculative, but I should explain that one basis for this analysis of the personal dimension is the attempt to uncover the aspects of an individual person that would have to persist if we are to be able to speak of the continued existence of a person after death in any significant sense. I am not here asserting that there is such an after-life; for the purposes of this study we can be agnostic about this, as about so many other claims. But the mainstream tradition is committed to an account of the person which makes a continued life a possibility, and given such a possibility I hold that an analysis along the lines that I have attempted is demanded. Another basis for this analysis is the attempt to describe the elements of the person from the moral point of view, that is, as the subject of strictly moral praise and blame. Here change cannot be achieved, as it can with bodily change, merely by the appropriate movement of causal factors. It is not merely that we have a complex system, as if changing the person were like the problem of reprogramming a very large computer, which required a massive analysis before we achieved the correct arrangement of parts. Personal change must involve the active participation of the agent.

It is worth pointing out here that the foregoing account of man is an attempt to describe his nature 'from below', if we use a distinction made at the end of the third section of the introduction. The grounds for suggesting that these five elements are included in our understanding of the self are human experiences. However, a complete Christian philosophy must also attempt to combine such an approach with one 'from above', in which man's essential nature is seen in the context of God's creative work as a whole. For example, in the first part of Aquinas' *Summa Theologiae*, the account of man comes after the accounts of the creation of angels and of matter, as of a being who in some way embodies a coming together of these two principles. This way of approaching the nature of man might be able to open up further insights.

To return to the analysis 'from below'. In the Aristotelian tradition moral change meant change in dispositions, the second of the suggested elements. I think that it is reasonable to look for the most striking effects of personal change here, but I am optimistic enough to believe that change here can produce fundamental changes in other aspects of the person, perhaps by the opening up of the potentialities of an original endowment. Nowhere, however, does it seem proper to think of personal change being enforced, by other men or by God, without the co-operation of the person himself.

This emphasis on personal participation can be so stressed that the ideal man becomes the total master of himself, like the Stoic

hero, unchanged within himself by any event in the outside world,
even by the torture of his own body or the intense suffering of his
friends. But this is not the ideal of the Christian tradition which,
as in so many other instances, treads a path between two extremes.
In the Christian tradition, men are not islands, to use Donne's
splendid simile, but parts of continents. They have an essential
inner core, plus an essential openness, so that the picture of
personal change as an inner process evoked or triggered by external events is still an inadequate one, based on an atomic conception of the person. It does less than justice to persons whose
fulfilment includes a relationship with others that is neither like
the merging of drops into an ocean, nor, at the other extreme,
like a chain linking two atoms. We truly find ourselves only when
we lose ourselves, in abandoning the selfish ego. 'Unless a grain
of wheat falls into the earth and dies, it remains alone.'[29]

The position that I am attempting to describe is similar to that
defended by John Oman in his *Grace and Personality*.[30] Here,
too, there is a strong emphasis on the self-determination of the
person, plus a contrast between the 'individuals' which most men
are, and the 'persons' they are meant to become when they realize
full relationships with others. Most striking of all is Oman's insistence that God's dealing with persons must respect their integrity as self-determining agents.

In the last chapter I indicated the kind of philosophy of physical
nature that was demanded by a doctrine of providence in that
order. Now it is beginning to be clear what account of man is
demanded by a doctrine of providence in the human order. There
has to be not only a basic freedom, so that it is meaningful to talk
of self-determining agents, but there has also to be an openness
of the self to the environment, especially to the environment
constituted by other persons and God, which makes interaction
at the personal level, and consequent personal change, possible.

There is a systematic difficulty here in finding an adequate
analogy for the human situation, precisely because the claim is
that we have before us a level of existence that emerges only with
the person. An analogy of a kind is provided by the example of
the first fishes that struggled on to the land as the oceans began
to shrink in prehistoric times, and lived, as it were, in two dimensions, that of the sea and that of the land, and were probably not
completely at home in either. Similarly the Christian philosophy
of man is of a hybrid creature, who is part of the natural order,
but who is struggling to emerge into the spiritual order of person-

hood. But it is not as if God *could* have made us members of the spiritual order directly; the very concept of a human person is linked with emergence from the natural order, an emergence that is chosen and struggled for by the person as he responds to grace.

In this context of the emergence of the person from the animal level to a new and higher level, the doctrine of evolution, far from being an embarrassment to Christian philosophy, should be seen as highly instructive and illuminating.

In man, therefore, we find a strange blend of the self-directing agent and the social self that finds itself only in relationship with others. It seems then that to the five elements that I claimed to be parts of the concept of a person I must add a sixth, namely a set of relationships which are in part *constitutive* of the person. This element, moreover, is open to voluntary change, and can be the source of change in other aspects of the person.

In the context of this philosophy of man it is possible to give an account of how providence can be held to work in the human order. There are four areas to consider: (1) General providence working indirectly, that is, through the natural order; (2) Special providence working indirectly; (3) General providence working strictly at the personal level; (4) Special providence working strictly at the personal level.

(1) It has often been claimed that the physical order in general is such as to encourage not only human evolution, as some of the writers discussed in the last chapter stressed, but also moral and spiritual growth. For example, over-eating tends to produce ill-health; and there are countless other examples of 'natural punishments' which have been seen as part of the design or government of the created order. An objector might reasonably point out that the presence of these 'natural punishments' has another very simple explanation, namely, the intimate connection between moral principles and survival. Indeed 'over-eating', as opposed to 'feasting', is conceptually linked with 'ill-health', which is in turn linked with the non-survival of the individual. More subtle moral ideas are often linked with group survival, as is courage. The Christian, if he is wise, will in no way deny these connections, but he will interpret them as one of the ways in which the natural order is designed to encourage and promote certain moral traits. In particular, the social pressures which encourage virtues linked with group survival tend to encourage men to be more open and less egocentric. It follows, however, that instances of 'natural punishment' are not evidence for providence; they are, rather, examples

of the providential order for one who already believes in providence.

(2) If God wills individual events in the physical world, either by the action of special providence or by miracle, the purpose, presumably, is not just for the sake of producing a natural effect, but of influencing man, or at least of producing the conditions in which man can be changed. Paul's rescue from shipwreck could be considered as an example of both. The centurion was changed in himself, and Paul was preserved so that he could be the future source of change in others.[31]

(3) The action of general providence working directly on persons, rather than through the intermediary of nature, does not have to include the idea of a personal God. For example, Plato's Idea of the Good, as interpreted in the analogy of the sun, illuminates all souls that are willing to respond to spiritual light by exerting a sort of pressure on the soul whenever it turns towards the good. The enlightenment that resulted entailed far more than the acquisition of knowledge, in the modern sense of that term, for it involved the drawing of the soul upwards until it became ready to live in the eternal order. Some other religious ideas are similar; for example, the Hindu doctrine of *karma* expresses the idea of a universal spiritual principle whereby what can be considered an impersonal force moulds the soul in response to the way it acts. The soul's status is inevitably changed, by a kind of causal law, as it follows after good or evil.

Up to a point the Christian tradition can allow the existence of equivalent spiritual forces of a general or impersonal kind, but it is bound to stress the limitations of such forces because of the claim that all men need Christ. Thus Aquinas, who is a representative of both Catholic and Protestant traditions at this point, claims that (1) unfallen man, while capable of fulfilling the whole moral law outwardly, could not fulfil the law with perfect love without grace; (2) fallen man can neither show perfect love, nor actually fulfil all the outward acts, without grace.[32] The emphasis therefore moves to the assistance of God made available in acts of special providence.

(4) Although the work of Christ does not exhaust the activity of special providence in the human order, because there is, for example, the inspiration of the Old Testament prophets (and liberal Christians would certainly allow for God's providential work in many non-Christian religions), it is the key to the Christian philosophy, especially when Christ is given a cosmic interpret-

ation. Christ is then the eternal 'Word', and through him even the Old Testament prophets were held to be inspired before the birth of Jesus.

This emphasis on the role of Christ led, and still leads, to obvious problems. What is to be said of those who do not know him, or could not know him? This latter class includes not only Old Testament heroes like Elijah and Enoch, who were said to have been translated to heaven, but Gentile philosophers like Socrates who were highly esteemed by the early Christians.

There have been various responses to the issue, and the more liberal among the Christians have always found it possible to open the doors to all sorts of people who were not or are not officially Christian, either by the doctrine of the invisible church, whose membership only God knows, or by the doctrine of the cosmic Christ already referred to. There is certainly some New Testament support for those doctrines, for example in the *logos* teaching of John's gospel,[33] and most of all in the parable of the great assize. The righteous are surprised at finding themselves on the right hand of the king, but the explanation is then given to them by the king himself. 'I was hungry, and you gave me food, I was thirsty and you gave me drink, I was a stranger, and you welcomed me, I was naked, and you clothed me, I was sick, and you visited me, I was in prison and you came to me.' When the righteous are still puzzled he goes on, 'As you did it to one of the least of these my brethren, you did it to me.'[34]

If this parable is taken in isolation, we appear to have the suggestion that salvation is only a matter of good works. What, then, is the role of providence in salvation? We cannot answer this question, from the point of view of the Christian tradition, without an examination of the doctrine of the atonement, and its relation to the concept of providence.

5. *The work of atonement*

It would go far beyond the scope of this book to provide a comprehensive account of atonement doctrine, but the ground has been prepared for two insights into what the Christian tradition has understood by atonement. These insights into the atonement are important for the concept of providence because they are directly concerned with the question of how God can effect change in persons.

The first insight relates to the theme of being drawn towards

something by love. We have found this idea in both Plato and
Aristotle. Here the role of *eros* was especially important because
it enabled them to postulate change in the things that were drawn,
but changelessness in the object that drew things. Christianity has
a doctrine that is clearly influenced by this, both in the general
idea of God as the final object of the human search for fulfilment,
and more specifically in the role of the cross, which draws men by
the demonstration of love. 'When I am lifted up,' John reports
Jesus as saying, 'I will draw all men to myself.'[35] There are,
however, at least two significant differences between this use of
love in the doctrine of the atonement and that of Plato and
Aristotle. First, the drawing of men involved an actual event in
history as well as the permanent fact of the love of God, and this
event made a change at least in the experience of Jesus. Second,
the Christian word for love, *agape*, has rather different connota-
tions from the *eros* of the philosophers, and is definitely more
suggestive of a personal relationship. Nevertheless, there is a
resemblance between the beauty that draws men in Plato's *Symposium* and the example of love that draws men in the New
Testament.

   This insight into the role of the cross in bringing about personal
change is the basis for one particular theory of the atonement, a
theory especially associated with Abelard. Here Christ's work is
seen principally in terms of its power to elicit a response of love
from the believer, a power that enables him to respond to God
and to receive grace. Even though this approach was little used
as a *theory* of the atonement in most periods of the church's
history, it has always expressed the devotion to the passion of
Christ at the popular level, and this fact indicates that it was of
great influence in the thinking of many ordinary Christians.[36]

   While at the level of the ordinary Christian this approach may
have sufficed for an explanation of the work of Christ, at the level
of theological speculation it has seemed inadequate to most theologians, including Abelard, because it tends to see the work of
Christ in subjective terms rather than as an objective historical
event. Even if being drawn by the example of Christ's love has a
powerful effect on the soul, most theologians have felt that this
could not be sufficient to overcome the grip of sin, and therefore
they have sought to make Christ's death a cosmic event, as dramatic on the spiritual level as the act of creation was on the
physical level. This was particularly the case in the Western,
Roman Catholic, branch of the church, as opposed to the Eastern

Orthodox churches, for the theologians of the West tended to stress the death of Christ more strongly than those of the East, who saw the death more as the final event in the whole earthly life of Christ, with a consequent emphasis on the incarnation.

The desire to find a theory that is adequate for the work of Christ as a cosmic event has led to two principal types of what can be called 'objective' theories. The first is the substitution theory, based on the claim that Christ died in the place of the sinner, and thus paid the penalty demanded by justice, the second the victory theory, in terms of which Christ won a cosmic victory over the powers of evil which broke their hold over men. Both theories can be supported by the interpretation of a considerable array of New Testament texts. Historically the former is especially associated with Anselm and the latter with Luther.[37]

When understood as religious imagery, and as sources of religious devotion, both of these theories have obvious power, but when they claim to be *explanations* of how persons are changed, then they both run into considerable difficulties. If the exponent insists on their mysterious quality, which may be quite legitimate in some religious contexts, he cannot at the same time stress their explanatory power! The difficulties are felt particularly by those whom I have called liberal Christians. On the one hand, the Anselmian theory runs into various moral objections. Is it in fact just to accept the sacrifice of an innocent victim in order to atone for the misdeeds of another? How exactly does the acceptance of such a sacrifice change a person either morally or in some less easily understood spiritual way? On the other hand, the Lutheran theory runs into problems as soon as one sees language about the devil and his battalions as oblique references to the collective power of human wickedness.

It is not my purpose to dismiss these theories, and for the purposes of this study we can remain agnostic about their value; my point is that in terms of offering an explanation of how personal change of a new kind is made possible by the work of Christ, they do not make any advance on the first, or Abelardian, approach. This last named does, even if only in a 'subjective' way, make a significant attempt at an explanation, for the claim that we can be changed by the dramatic example of another's love is perfectly plausible in the light of ordinary human experience. On the other hand, the attempts I have read to explain the work of Christ as the victim who bore our sins do not take seriously enough the integrity of the moral person, and what I have described as the problem of genuine change within the person.

However, I have claimed that the analysis of the nature of change in persons can offer a second insight into the meaning of the atonement as an explanation of personal change. This arises from the emphasis on the essential openness of the person, so that relationships are in part constitutive of the person. Hence we have what I should claim to be a third kind of 'objective' theory, which can be supported by the New Testament, but which, unlike the other two, does have explanatory power.

Throughout the history of religious speculation, both in the East and in the West, there has been a constant danger either of overemphasizing our individuality at the expense of our social nature, or of stressing so strongly the way in which relationships constitute our nature that we lose any meaningful individuality. This is why I have suggested that the union of the person with others should be compared neither with a drop of water absorbed into an ocean (which reflects a typical Eastern metaphor) nor with a link between two atoms (which is the relationship implicit in much talk of personal salvation). A more satisfactory metaphor is rooted in the experience of the bond between two lovers, as suggested by the inclusion of the long love poem, the Song of Solomon, in the Hebrew and Christian Bibles. Given an emphasis on this kind of union, we can find room for an atonement doctrine based on a complex picture of human nature in which men can be seen either as individuals or as parts of a corporate whole. For example, our sins are our own fault, but in some way we share in the fallen state of the children of Adam. From the point of view of grace we are saved one by one as we respond to love, but only as 'members of the body of Christ'.

If we are prepared to take seriously the idea that the complete person cannot be properly defined except in terms that include his relationship with others, then the New Testament proclamation of a life which can share in the suffering, death, and risen life of Christ, can be considered as an *explanation* of personal change, provided that one also believes that a personal relationship with Jesus is possible.

Here I must once again stress that I am writing not only for Christians, and that in these first six chapters I am seeking an understanding of the meaning of providence. Therefore for many readers, the possibility I have just referred to will be the theoretical possibility that a follower of Jesus may be able to enter into a relationship with a person who, in one sense, died two thousand years ago, and that this relationship can be so significant for the very being of the Christian that it is the source of personal change. Whether one holds that such a relationship is actually possible will depend on one's religious beliefs, but in order to understand what the Christian *means* by atonement we have to consider the possibility, without any necessary commitment to what can actually happen. This is another example of what I have described as the need for an act of sympathetic understanding, if we are to be able to comprehend what a concept means within a certain tradition. We need such acts of sympathy to understand not only religious concepts, but also many other concepts within traditions or cultures different from our own.

To return to the New Testament, one of the strongest statements of the approach to the atonement that I have been outlining reads as follows:

> Do you not know that all of us who have been baptized into Christ Jesus were baptized into his death? We were buried therefore with him by baptism into death, so that as Christ was raised from the dead by the glory of the Father, we too might walk in a newness of life . . . But if we have died with Christ, we believe that we shall also live with him.[38]

This passage can be supplemented with many more, where the emphasis is on the 'new creation' in Christ, or the experience of life 'in Christ', or sharing in the sufferings of Christ, or celebrating unity with Christ in the breaking of bread.[39] There can be no understanding of what the Christian *means* by atonement without an attempt to understand this sense of a life in fellowship with Christ, and with others in Christ, that runs throughout the New Testament and reflects what was for the participants an experience of incredible power. Given such an understanding, then the transformation of the person by incorporation into such a fellowship is perfectly coherent. Personal responsibility, and the need for personal suffering, are not avoided, but rather stressed, for it is claimed that we have to suffer with Christ as we die to the 'old man' within us and experience his compassion for others; but the possibilities for personal change are given a new dimension by seeing this suffering in the context of relationship with others.

In order to conclude this section, two further comments on the Christian doctrine of the incarnation are called for.[40] First, an adequate account, in terms of a doctrine of atonement, of how

man can be changed inseparably linked with an adequate account
of the one who does the atoning. It is doubtful whether the
'objective' theory of the atonement that I have outlined can be
seriously entertained, except in the context of a doctrine of the
incarnation which goes beyond that offered by the more radical
exponents of a revised Christian theology. It is not that all the
orthodox language about Jesus as 'the second person of the Trinity' is essential for an adequate Christian philosophy, but a claim
that the incarnation represented a divine *initiative* of a new kind
is essential. Thus, the sorts of theory proposed in the recent *The
Myth of God Incarnate*[41] seem to me to be inadequate as the basis
for any Christian philosophy within the tradition with which I
have been concerned, since on these views the *birth* of Jesus
cannot be held to be a significant act of divine intervention; consequently, the vital relationship of 'in Christ' is robbed of the
possibility of opening up a new opportunity for human change. I
would advocate much more agnosticism in Christian philosophy
concerning the exact relationship of Jesus to God, coupled with
an insistence that as '*the* image of the invisible God in human
form' (Paul's language[42]), Jesus represented, from his birth, the
decision by a personal God to identify himself with mankind. This
act of identification meant accepting human weakness and vulnerability, including the weakness manifested in a baby and the
vulnerability to death. Further, given the human situation in general and the social scene of the time in particular, this initiative
was bound to involve the eventual killing of the man who bore
the divine image, though whether this would be by crucifixion, or
by some other way, was not determined, nor determinable, in
advance.

Second, if we refer back to the difference between the approaches 'from below' and 'from above', which has been mentioned twice before, any adequate attempt to understand what
Christians have meant by the incarnation must take account of
both approaches. On the one hand, the historical nature of incar-
national claims demands that there be reference to the human
experience of Jesus, and to reflection upon that experience (the
approach 'from below'). On the other hand, if Jesus is claimed to
be the image of God, an image that reflects him in some unique
or extraordinary way, then there must also be reference to the
concept of God. In traditional Christian theology, this has taken
place through the ideas of the procession of the Son and of the
Spirit, and the idea of the external creation being through the Son

(the approach 'from above'). Accordingly, in Aquinas' *Summa Theologiae*, Christ is considered in part three, after the consideration of God and of man, as the principle that draws the two together.

6. Providence and evil

If man is under the government of God (and any doctrine of providence must assert this to be true in some sense), is God then the author of evil? This is one of the notorious questions that any consideration of God's activity has to face. The mainstream Christian tradition has a well-worn answer which I shall summarize very briefly, and then I shall attempt to go one step further in the light of the analysis undertaken so far.

It is customary to contrast two kinds of evil, moral and natural. Moral evil consists in the deliberate choice of something less than the good, and is possible only for rational beings possessed of free-will. Given the existence of such beings, the possibility of evil is an inescapable one, unless one accepts the argument of J. L. Mackie, that it would have been logically possible for God to have made free beings who always, as a matter of fact, chose what is good.[43] However, given the human environment in which millions of human beings are interacting, it is doubtful whether such a possibility is even a logical one. I have already argued that it is not necessarily the case that all desirable options are open to providence, and I suspect that, even if there were only two human beings in the world, providence *could not* always contrive situations where they naturally chose the good. Thus, for most Christian philosophers, once there are living examples of what can be counted as human beings, evil becomes a logical possibility and a practical certainty. Further, given the essential openness of man that I have stressed, the evil of one man, like the good, will inevitably affect others. Nevertheless, a universe in which there are men, with both evil and redemption within it, may be a better universe than one with no men in it at all. Therefore God cannot be condemned for the existence of evil, and he can be dismissed as less than omnipotent only if one uses 'omnipotent' to mean the power to do literally anything. Christians have rarely meant this, and I do not believe that such a concept can be made coherent.

Natural or physical evil concerns the pain and ugliness found in the physical order, especially animal suffering and that part of human suffering which is not attributable to moral evil. The traditional apology has already been referred to and is similar to the apology concerning moral evil, in that stress is laid on the autonomy of man in the one case and on the autonomy of the physical order in the other. Man's personal life demands that he live in a world where the consequences of his actions are generally predictable, and this can be only in a law-like and law-abiding world. Again, therefore, God cannot be condemned if the existence of pain is a pre-condition of any truly human existence. This is a line of argument that will have added force if one accepts the recommendation I have made that Christians should stop saying 'It is God's will' when some extraordinary and unhappy event occurs. Likewise, I think that there is a sort of blasphemy involved in the insurance companies' use of the phrase 'acts of God'. It is a naive belief in the total capacity of providence to effect anything and everything in the world, that helps more than anything else to arouse questions concerning the problem of evil in both its forms.

The mainstream tradition sees the relationship of providence and evil along such lines, and for those who accept a doctrine of free-will it has often seemed adequate. However, given the distinction that I have made between general and special providence, the problem can still reappear, though in a rather more subtle form. The apology just given fits very well with a conception of general providence, concerned with the over-all production of a suitable environment for human life and growth; but if there is also a special providence, which steers some specific events, why, many believers and unbelievers may ask, does not this special providence show itself more frequently when there are conditions of terrible distress? This is a real dilemma for many religious people in moments of crisis. If there is only an impersonal governor, then there is no intellectual problem produced by the existence of evil; but if a personal God is manifested in acts of special providence, why, the sufferer will ask, is he not manifested here and now? This is not a 'knock-down' argument, for the sufferer may be well aware that providence cannot do everything, and that he has no special right to be the beneficiary of special care; but it is a powerful and insidious argument, that gathers strength as the sufferer continues to look in vain for examples of God's personal concern. It is the negative side of the experiential argument that I outlined in the introduction; and just as I wrote then of a kind of verification of the personal hypothesis, so here there can be its falsification.

An analogy from legal philosophy can illustrate the problem.

The general laws of the state have, in a sense, to be impersonal, concerned with what will generally make for the common good. However, for the injustices that will inevitably arise, because of the general nature of laws, the law itself has a partial remedy, namely the principle of equity. From the time of Aristotle,[44] this has allowed for a special flexibility, so that the necessarily general character of laws should not unduly hurt the private citizen. Equity can be pleaded before the courts in most civilized nations, and relates to the statute law rather as special providence relates to general providence. The problem now reappears as follows. When a civilized court will treat an individual hard case with equity, even when the laws have to be general, why does not special providence more often assist the individual, even though the ordinary government of the world must be by general laws?

In this situation many intelligent people do of course opt for the belief that there is no God, or no God that can be regarded as personal in any significant sense, thereby indicating that a kind of falsification of the religious personal hypothesis is indeed possible. But the mainstream tradition still has an important point to make that must be considered by the intelligent critic. This centres on the purpose of God within the created order.

From the point of view of human beings there is a general purpose in life, namely happiness, either explicitly or implicitly expressed in the goals they seek for most of the time. The perplexity they feel with regard to evil arises in the face of the frequent, and seemingly unnecessary, frustration of this happiness. But does the purpose of providence coincide with human purpose?

The Christian tradition must answer both yes and no to this question. Yes, in that God's ultimate purpose for man is a happiness that passes man's understanding: as the *Westminster Confession* puts it, 'Man's chief end is to glorify God, and to enjoy him for ever.'[45] No, in that the immediate sources of man's happiness may be irrelevant to, and sometimes inimical to, this intended happiness, a happiness that only the good can realize. Therefore the *immediate* plan by which the human order is providentially governed has more to do with the development of the person as a person than with happiness. This does not entail that happiness is unimportant in the short run, for it is not only a good in itself, it is also one of the formative factors in the shaping of the person. Nevertheless, happiness is not the sole yardstick.

From this point of view, the problem of suffering looks rather

Providence

different; and perhaps some of those who think they have falsified all providential claims have merely been applying a criterion centred on their search for private happiness. What is called for by one who believes in providence is not necessarily the removal of misfortune, though this removal may be a possibility, but grace to come through it in a way that makes him more of a person. This, I suspect, is the clue to that otherwise puzzling last request in the Lord's prayer, 'Bring us not to the test, but deliver us from evil.'[46] (The more familiar, but misleading, translation is 'Lead us not into temptation.') The Christian prays that he may not be brought to the situation where he will be tested. This is a natural human request that even Jesus expressed, ('Father, if thou be willing, remove this cup from me.'[47]). However, if the test has to come, because this is just the way things are going to work out, then the Christian prays for grace to act rightly.[48]

VI

Providence and History

1. Providence and the Old Testament

Of the three areas that I have separated for comment, nature, man, and history, it is history that has usually been held to manifest the work of providence most forcefully. The orders of nature and of man have continued much as before from century to century, but history witnesses enormous, and probably irreversible, changes, which many see as the unfolding of a master plan. Moreover, any such plan can hardly be a human one, for with rare exceptions, like Alexander the Great, men have not tried to mould history by their own efforts. On traditional Christian views the plan must be the work of providence. Collingwood describes the reasoning as follows.

> Human action . . . is actuated *a tergo* by immediate and blind desire . . . Desire is not the tamed horse of Plato's metaphor, it is a runaway horse and the sin . . . into which it leads us is not a sin which we deliberately choose to commit, it is an inherent and original sin proper to our nature. From this it follows that the achievements of man are due not to his own proper forces of will and intellect, but to something other than himself.[1]

On such a view history provides both a scene and evidence for the work of providence.

The Christian view of history is centred on an interpretation of biblical history. How far non-biblical history demonstrates the work of providence is a matter of controversy among Christians, as we shall see. Biblical history, moreover, is especially concerned with the interpretation of the Old Testament, both because of the long period involved and because it is seen as the preparation for the New Testament. However, in order to make a rational assessment of Old Testament history we have to recognize the fact that what we read is not 'straight' history (with the interesting exception of the court history of David and Solomon), but an interpretation of history that is already seen as providential. To some extent it is true of all historical writing that what we are presented with is not straight fact, but fact along with interpretation, for otherwise history could not be written at all. There has at least to be a selection of material in terms of what is considered relevant and important, and this selection implies a series of interpretative judgments that make it hard to say exactly what 'straight' history is. Nevertheless, there is certainly a sharp contrast between modern historical writing and that of the Old Testament writers, because the latter were writing from a particular standpoint that gives to the Old Testament an extraordinary unity, despite the great variety of its writings. This unity arises because the first covenant, or 'testament', believed to have been made between God and the Jews, immediately after the exodus from Egypt, was seen as the centrepiece for all the writings. Much of the text concerns its exposition; the rest is either leading up to it, or interpreting later history in terms of it, or meditating upon its meaning.

The result of this is that, if we are to appreciate what the Old Testament means for those within the tradition we are concerned with, whatever our views as to what actually happened, we have to read the text with the assumption that at least certain key portions of the Jewish tradition are real history. In particular, this applies to the deliverance from Egypt, the actual covenant made at Sinai, and the bringing of the chosen people into the promised land. However, even within such a sympathetic reading, it is not necessary that every detail be accepted as literally accurate, for within the tradition itself there are misgivings and rival interpretations of many specific events.

The traditional interpretation of these key events clearly involves special providence, for God's choice of Israel and of the prophets reflects acts of will that cannot be covered by an extension of general providence. Is miracle demanded as well? This is a hard question to answer with assurance, but I shall argue that the answer is no.

As we have seen, the distinction between special providence

and miracle is not a biblical one; it is one that arises only when a certain philosophy of nature as an order with its own laws comes into being. For the Old Testament writers, the key events were simply 'the marvellous acts' of God.[2] To translate such phrases by the word 'miracle' is already to adopt an interpretation that goes beyond the original thinking. However, for us the question of miracle is significant because we may want to know whether a sympathetic understanding of the Old Testament requires the belief that certain key events occurred which were in principle inexplicable by natural means, or whether all the key events could be classed as events that fell under special providence. This is a specially important question for those who doubt whether miracles are the means by which God works, or whether they ever occur.

There is no doubt that the story surrounding the three key events is laced with accounts which, if taken literally, would demand the word 'miracle'. However, none of these miraculous happenings is essential to the key events themselves. Thus, according to one account, the crossing of the Red Sea was explained by a strong east wind. Again, the terms of the first covenant were the result of Moses' communing with God on the mountain, and his formulation of the Ten Commandments certainly does not require miracle. When, in a famous biblical epic, a laser-like finger of God actually engraved the stone tablets, many people watching the film felt that a convincing scene of an old man meditating on what kind of law to give the people was suddenly rendered absurd. Yet again, the route to the promised land involved a forty-year wandering, in which at least one battle was lost,[3] and this too does not require miracle. It is in fact utterly congruous with other examples of the early history of peoples, when great hardship and adventure were experienced, that in later ages men look back to this period, and in looking back magnify the actual events and interpret them as clues to the real meaning of a culture.

2. The nature of providential action in history

If from within the Christian tradition the three key events under discussion do not demand miracle, but do demand providence, what can we say about this providential activity? The answer must take into account the fact that the government of history is through the government of nature and of man, so that there is a kind of discontinuity between the treatment of nature and of man on the one hand, and of history on the other. According to the tradition, nature can be governed directly by providence, and so can men, even if this government has to be by persuasion. However, a piece of history is not a substance, apart from the pieces of nature and of the human beings that are involved, so that it seems meaningless to talk of God's *direct* action on history. Action must be through nature or man. Moreover, the emphasis must be on man, for although a natural occurrence like an earthquake can influence history, it can be of historical interest only in so far as people are involved who are forced to react to the occurrence. The earthquakes of the Cambrian age are not part of our history.

This introduces the next important question. I have argued that, where man is concerned, providence does not necessitate events, but acts by persuasion, on the grounds that only an interpretation along these lines will make sense when the tradition is understood in the contemporary context. This must at least be the case when men are treated as moral agents, and not as Sherlock's 'instruments of providence'. But since history is concerned with human acts, how far can history be governed, or its plan *determined*? In earlier times most Christians would undoubtedly have insisted that in some manner at least the key events in history were providentially determined in detail. I shall refer to this as 'the old view', and shall argue that if this means that the details of the events concerned were laid down in the divine mind before they happened, such determination is not necessary for an account of providence in history. In fact the view that providence works by a detailed determination of events is detrimental to a proper understanding of providence in history. Thus whereas in the case of the Old Testament miracles one may well be agnostic about the view according to which sacred history is studded with the miraculous, in the case of the general government of history I am opposed to the old view that God lays down exactly who will do what.

Let us begin this discussion with a consideration of the role of general providence in history. Many historical events can be given an interpretation in terms of a general providence, which may or may not be personally conceived. Once again the tidal analogy is helpful. Through a continuing 'pressure' on nature or man a long-term movement could be determined without the detailed determination of each event, provided that sufficient numbers were involved. To take an example of a pressure on history through the natural order, human civilization has tended to move from a hunting culture to a farming culture to a city-based culture, in part, at least, in response to a pressure on food resources. As populations grew, a more and more efficient system of the management and distribution of resources became imperative. One cannot prove that this is the work of providence; but if the providential plan was to produce an increasingly complex social system, which could then be the context for various kinds of advance, intellectual, artistic, and spiritual, then the government of history towards this complexity could well be seen as an example of providential activity. But, as with Kant's marriage statistics, no single event is determined, only the overall pattern. To take an example of a pressure on history through the human order, there is a universal curiosity or sense of wonder built into the human race; for, as Aristotle put it, 'All men by nature desire to know.'[4] This has led to all sorts of personal enquiries, but gradually, and perhaps inevitably, it has led eventually to a scientific examination of nature, history, language, and so on. For a man of faith this, too, can be an example of providence at work, for we have now not only a complex social system, but a developing intelligence as a context for the work of special providence.

Even if some of the biblical events cannot be explained along these lines, general providence is an important element in any discussion of the providential ordering of history as a whole. This is given added force when we see that many of the special events could be included in the government of general providence, in accordance with illustrations from catastrophe theory like those already mentioned. Athens in the classical period, and Florence during the Renaissance, witnessed an incredible number of geniuses within a short period. It is ridiculous to put down these cultural explosions to the fortuitous arrival of a few hundred men of genius all at the same time, and quite unnecessary to introduce the miraculous; rather, one must say that the cultural and economic conditions triggered off an explosion which had long been prepared for by the build-up of artistic and intellectual forces. There are always more geniuses around than we realize, but it takes the right environment to enable most of them to flourish. Thus the explosion is in a way parallel to the earthquake in the natural order, and some conversions in the human order, in that the sudden discontinuity can mislead us into supposing that fantastic factors must be at work. Extending this approach, one can point to the extraordinary spiritual and moral development that seems to have occurred in many parts of the world around the sixth and fifth centuries BC, evidenced in men like the Buddha,

Lao Tsu, Confucius, Zoroaster, and a number of Hebrew prophets, including Second Isaiah and Jeremiah. We now know that there was more contact and cross-fertilization between distant cultures than was formerly realized, and one is tempted to see this world-wide spiritual explosion as a response to various moral and spiritual pressures that had been building up all over the world, though of their nature we know little. In this case we find, once again, that it is possible to talk of providence without its being necessary or desirable that the details of each event be laid down.[5]

Let us turn now to a consideration of special providence. When God acts on history through the order of man, the analysis offered in Chapter V demands that providence work by persuasion, so that once again the details of each event need not, and for the most part cannot, be determined. But does this make it possible for God to be the 'Lord of history'? Can the key events in the scriptures, like the three surrounding the first covenant, be so interpreted that the details are not enforced by a coercive providence, and yet in a significant way still lie under divine government? The answer is 'yes', provided that we are prepared to apply the kind of analysis proposed for the betrayal by Judas to all the other crucial episodes. For example, take the selection of Moses as the leader of the exodus. The time was ripe, and he was a suitable choice. But if I am right, there is a significant sense in which Moses could have refused, or have hesitated even longer. He did in fact hesitate, according to the book of Exodus, and this itself is an interesting pointer to a surprising historical candour, given the time of writing.[6] If he had done either of these things, history would have been different in some details, but even if he had refused utterly, perhaps the sweep of history would have been much the same. This all depends on one's point of view. On the 'great man' theory of history, a decision by one key person could transform history, but Marxist and Christian theories, despite many differences, have in common a belief that the forces that make for change in the long run are to be found elsewhere: in the material and class conditions for the Marxist, in these conditions plus others, including the influence of God, for the contemporary Christian. However, over a period of time the influence of God, if present, could be decisive; for if Moses had said 'no', some other leader would have been found; and although Moses's character involved a style that must have left a permanent mark on history, an exodus of a similar kind could have taken place without him.

(This allusion to the mark left by a person is important in order to dispel the notion that someone's refusal to accept a role really does not matter, since 'it will all be the same anyway'. On a Christian view, God will still achieve his long-term purpose despite a man's refusal to co-operate, but not only will history be different in the short run (perhaps with terrible consequences for some people), there will also be a slight change in its long-run character, and an opportunity to make us of the 'style' that was mentioned in Chapter V as part of a person's natural endowment may be gone for ever.)

Although the freedom that I am proposing for Moses would have startled the Old Testament writers, this approach is not only demanded by an adequate Christian philosophy of man; it is even suggested by many of the experiences of the Old Testament heroes as these are preserved in the text. To put it crudely, God had trouble with many of his chosen leaders. Moses did not want to be a speaker, Saul was disobedient, David adulterous, Solomon polytheistic, Jonah obstinate and bad-tempered, Jeremiah easily dispirited, and so on. How many others perhaps were called to be leaders, although we never hear of them because they succeeded in refusing the roles that providence had designed for them? The hesitations we know about do not suggest the experience of a God who dictates who will be a prophet and exactly what he shall say; they rather support the claim that God should not be conceived as a coercive source of human action, even in key moments of history. Divine rule over men and over history need not be of this kind. Indeed, an analysis of this sort should be applied even to the events surrounding the incarnation, for a large part of the significance of Mary is the fact that she accepted the role that was demanded of her, 'Behold the handmaid of the Lord: let it be to me according to your word.'[7] In the old view these words signified an obedient submission to the role that had been thrust upon her, but I am suggesting a reinterpretation in which the role itself was accepted by her. Such a view fits better with our experience of choice, it fits better with an adequate philosophy of man, and it is sufficient to give meaning to providential action in history.

3. History, sacred and secular

The three events that I have isolated as crucial for the Old Testament are obviously not the only examples of providential guidance within biblical history, as this is understood within the

Christian tradition. To fill out the picture we need a scheme involving four principal stages.

First, there is the period before the exodus. This comprises the story of Adam and his descendants, setting the scene in terms of the human condition in general, followed by the story of Abraham and his descendants, setting the scene in terms of the prehistory of the Jewish tribes. For the purposes of the second stage it is not essential that these episodes be historical, even though as a matter of fact the Abraham stories almost certainly contain some ancient oral tradition. What matters is the symbolism of Adam (the Hebrew word both for 'mankind' and for 'earth') and of Abraham (who became the symbol of faith).

Second, there is the period of the exodus, centred on the three events discussed. Here a kernel of historical truth is demanded by the mainstream tradition, though there are existentialist Christians and some other radicals who would regard this as unimportant.

Third, there is the period from the exodus to the end of the Old Testament. Here, among other writings, we have in the court history of David and Solomon (contrary to what Collingwood asserts[8]), the first humanistic historical writing that we know about, with the heroes depicted more or less as they were, 'warts and all', and a new concern for human history as such. In contrast, however, most of this history is written from a very particular point of view, based on the prophetic interpretation of history. The prophets claimed that the whole of Jewish history manifested the judgment of God. When people sinned they suffered; when they obeyed all went well. Thus the exile was seen as a punishment, and the return from exile as both an act of divine mercy and a reward for faithfulness. Obedience to the covenant, especially in its prohibition of idolatry and in its moral demands, was the clue to divine protection, and the whole of history demonstrated this. The ten northern tribes were virtually destroyed around 722 BC, only a tiny fragment of Samaritans ever returning, and this was the supreme example of divine displeasure with the chosen people.[9]

In the main, this prophetic interpretation of history is bound to seem unrealistic to the modern reader. We may admire the moral eloquence, and especially the increasing concern with the oppression of the poor, which preoccupied the later prophets, but as an explanation of why there was plenty or misery, or why battles were won or lost, it seems quite inadequate. Many of the Old Testament writers evidently sensed this, and consequently they

agonized over the suffering of the innocent and the flourishing of
the wicked. If we look at non-biblical history in terms of a moral
evaluation, with hindsight it appears that many of the great battles
of history were won by the wrong side, for example the battle of
Bosworth, the siege of Warsaw, and the victories of every invading
army. Similarly, if we knew more about the background to the
battles of biblical history, we should probably make the same kind
of judgment. To the outsider, for example, Joshua's invasion of
Canaan, and the slaughter of women and children that accom-
panied it, looks like the invasion of most other invading armies.
The fact, if it is a fact, that he believed that he was obeying God's
command is no more justification for such atrocities than Hitler's
belief that he was fulfilling the historic role of Germany.

However, the inadequacy of the prophetic interpretation of
history does not prove that Jewish history was not providential
after the exodus; it merely shows that providence is not primarily
concerned with political and worldly success, to be meted out in
proportion to one's deserts. Thus the Christian can still see a
purpose in Jewish history in terms of the preparation of a culture
for the coming of the Messiah. This is much more in accord with
the Christian's experience of God in his own time (for God does
not seem to be specially interested in our wars), and it is also in
accord with the insight of some of the later prophets. In Second
Isaiah, for example, we see the purpose of Israel, not in terms of
a successful nation, but in terms of 'the light to lighten the Gentiles'[10], a role which was to involve the suffering of God's servant.[11]
Thus for the Christian tradition, periods one, two, and three were
all preparations for the New Testament drama, which is the content of the fourth period. Here, for any recognizably Christian
philosophy, at least a kernel of strictly historical events is essential.

The foregoing has been a summary of the traditional view of
the relationship of providence to biblical history. Even more difficult and controversial is the relationship to the rest of history.
As a first step, in order to concentrate on essentials, we should
perhaps set apart those portions of non-Hebrew history that directly bear upon biblical history; for here the biblical tradition
certainly asserts that they must fall under divine guidance.[12] What
are we to say of the rest, especially of that which is often called
'secular' or 'profane'? In general I prefer not to use these expressions, nor the contrasting 'sacred', because of the ambiguity involved. For example, does sacred history include the historical
events surrounding other religions, like Muhammad's flight from

Mecca? Does it include church history? Does it include events
which, sociologically speaking, are almost if not absolutely indis-
tinguishable from religious events in the ordinary sense, like Marxist martyrdoms? In addition to the ambiguity evident from these
questions, the very contrast of 'sacred' and 'secular' already suggests that a radically different treatment of certain parts of history
is called for, whereas many religious thinkers think that all history
is essentially a unity. My policy, therefore, will be to avoid these
terms from now on, except when discussing thinkers who use
them, notably Vico, and use the much clearer distinction between
biblical and non-biblical history. In doing this we need not assume
that different laws must govern biblical history from those that
govern the rest of history. Whether biblical history differs from
the rest of history only as English history differs from the rest of
history is one way of putting the question that must now be faced.

There are several answers to this question from within the
Christian tradition. One view denies that there is any radical gulf
between biblical and non-biblical history, because God is equally
Lord of all historical events. At the opposite extreme we find a
complete separation of biblical and non-biblical history, based on
the claim that biblical history is providentially ordained, whereas
the rest of history is a directionless and chaotic movement reflect-
ing material and personal forces that have no ultimate meaning.
Between these positions is an intermediate one which allows a
great measure of autonomy to history as a process that has its own
kinds of laws, congruous with the laws governing the natural and
human orders, but which also allows providential influence to
operate in the long run. I shall argue that the concept of providence can best be applied to history under a variation of this
intermediate view.

4. Direction, progress and judgment

In the discussion of providential action in history so far an important ambiguity has been glossed over. Does the providential
ordering of history suggest that it is directional, or progressive, or
simply that it is an arena for God's judgment? When people speak
of the 'meaning' of history, there is often a confusion between
interpretations of the meaning of history that are based on these
three factors.

In the case of biblical history the mainstream tradition would
assert providential ordering in all three senses. History was direc-

tional, at least from the time of Abraham, and this was perhaps the most important legacy of the biblical view for the interpretation of history by secular thinkers. Collingwood, for example, has pointed out the crucial difference between the directional view and that of the Greeks, for whom history was a circular process. On the directional view of history are built the philosophies of Hegel, Marx, and many others.[13] Within the Bible there is not only direction (that is, in terms of the preparation for the coming of the Messiah), there is also progress of a kind, namely, in the gradual understanding of the nature of God. Anthropomorphic terms like 'jealousy' are reinterpreted, and the emphasis on love grows. There is also belief in judgment, as we have seen.

So far as non-biblical history is concerned, the Bible itself leaves open the questions of direction and progress, except for the suggestion that Israel will become a light for the Gentiles, and for belief in a last day. However, there are clear indications that divine judgment is held to be operative everywhere. This is evident, for example, in the first two chapters of Amos, and in the suggestion that the divine servant will judge the Gentiles.[14] The same belief in a universal judgment in history reappears in Paul.[15]

Given that the foregoing describes the essentials of the biblical view, what sense can we make of it today? I shall carry over the questions relating to direction and progress in non-biblical history to the next section, and attempt here an assessment of providence in its role of judge within history.

In the last section I claimed that the prophetic interpretation of Jewish history was unrealistic 'in the main'. I added this saving clause because it is not unreasonable to see some long-term connection between morality and historical success, parallel to the sort of 'natural punishments' discussed in Chapter V which make for a rough and ready connection between personal morality and personal success. There is no mystery about this, for in the individual case there is the link, already referred to, between survival values and morality, and in the historical case there is the same link applicable to nations, evidenced in the fact that successful co-operation has as a precondition an element of morality. Plato pointed out that a successful gang of thieves could not avoid all elements of justice.[16]

The upshot of this is that, if one believes in providence, it is not unreasonable to see some long-term influence of this providence in history, in terms of a kind of judgment executed on nations, but only in the long run, and only in a very general way.

Experience does not support the view that, if there is a special
providence, its work is clearly manifest in history by acts of judgment on nations.

Behind this position there is a claim that needs to be spelled
out and defended. It is to the effect that it is proper to use our
contemporary experience when we seek to interpret the history
of the past, but with an important qualification. By way of illustration we can recall Thucydides, who was able to make more
sense of military history than any previous writer, not least because he had been a general and knew what was possible and
what was plausible in a military operation. Similarly, most people
with a minimum of horse-riding experience know that many West-
erns are pure fiction, among other reasons because horses cannot
gallop all night or even for a substantial part of a night. In general,
the rational assessment of events to which we have not been a
party, whether in the present or in the past, must include this kind
of judgment. However, the qualification arises in that there is a
great danger in this generally valid approach when we come to
something that is genuinely outside our experience, and *a fortiori*,
when an event is unique in kind. In such cases we can rely only
on our evaluation of the witnesses, and on the very difficult procedure of trying to assess how far the alleged happening is congruous with the rest of our experience and our over all philosophy.

It follows from this claim about the relevance of contemporary
experience that a rational evaluation of providential claims concerning the key events in biblical history is of a different kind
from the rational evaluation of the claim that there is a divine
judgment manifested in all history. The former concerns events
which, if they occurred, were either unique or extraordinarily
rare; and therefore it is hard to see how the historian, as historian,
can be other than agnostic about their historicity. He may make
relevant comments about, for example, the greater general reli-
ability of Mark's account compared with that of John, but it is
unreasonable to ask him to make a firm judgment on an allegedly
unique event. (In principle, the historian might come across evidence that falsified the resurrection story, or that amounted to
very strong counter-evidence; but there is great difficulty in saying
what strictly historical evidence could demonstrate the occurrence
of an event as out of the ordinary as the alleged resurrection,
given the fact that alternative interpretations of any historical
evidence are always possible.)

In contrast to the problem of the evaluation of unique events, the claim that there is a divine judgment manifested in history on the kingdoms of the world is a general claim, and *is* open to historical judgment. Moreover, apart from the rough and ready connection that has already been indicated, the verdict must be negative.

What, then, of providential interpretations of general history in terms of direction and progress? Before attempting an answer to these questions I shall review the answers given by Vico, one of the greatest of the philosophers of history. As in the case of Sherlock in Chapters IV and V, it is helpful, as an aid to clarification, to contrast what one holds to be an important but mistaken position with one that is held to be more adequate.

5. *Giambattista Vico and the 'new science' of history*

Vico made a radical separation between 'sacred' and 'secular' history, the former being exclusively the history of the Hebrews. The Hebrews, he held, were from the beginning a different species from the rest of men, had a different origin, and were under a direct and miraculous providential rule.[17] 'Besides the ordinary help from providence which was all that the gentiles had, the Hebrews had extraordinary help from the true God.'[18] For Vico this was more than the prejudice of a good Catholic, it was a conviction based on the phenomenon of Jewish history, with its extraordinary combination of antiquity and persistence. This excluded it, in his view, from the normal pattern that was exhibited in the rest of history.

The pattern which Vico held to be the common lot of the Gentile nations was that of a cycle. Essentially the cycle consisted of three periods, though in the detailed application of his scheme there are sub-divisions that make his history more complex than this suggests. The periods can be thought of as the ages of gods, of heroes, and of men, and these correspond to appropriate kinds of institution, language and law.[19] The cycle starts with a primitive form of barbarism, in which men see themselves as subject to a variety of gods; this is followed by a set of 'heroic' customs; and these in turn give way to more rationalized and civil ones. The climax is then inevitably followed by a relapse into a new kind of barbarism, and the whole cycle begins afresh. History, therefore, is a kind of spiral, with a similar cycle recurring in every nation, never returning to exactly the same state as before, but to a new variation on the same essential pattern.

Does this represent direction or progress? There are certainly both within each cycle; but is there either from an over all point of view? The general impression given by a careful reading of Vico is that there is not. The purpose of the whole system is the preservation of the human species, for the continued relapses into barbarism save mankind from destroying itself by the excesses of the civilized age of men.[20] This, however, is not 'progress', just a complicated way of maintaining the existence of the human species. There is a hint of a rather more optimistic possibility towards the end of the *New Science*, and the suggestion of some kind of final end to history, but this is not stressed at all in the main exposition.[21]

The two themes that I have expounded so far are (1) the radical separation of sacred and secular history, and (2) the cyclical process which is held to be empirically evident from the scientific study of history. The latter forms the basis of Vico's apparently extraordinary claim that the new science (i.e. history) provides a positive demonstration of the work of providence.

In order to understand the reasoning here we must first recall the old Christian view that God works through human passions, achieving things that man is ignorant of. This idea recurs in many forms, such as Hegel's account of the 'cunning of reason'. In Vico's theory there is a sense in which man makes history; indeed this is precisely why, according to him, history can be a science, for Vico insists that we can know to be true (*verum*) only what we have ourselves made (*factum*). On the local level history is evidently made by man; and even on a grand scale there is a sense in which it is man-made, for what happens is that God uses human irrationality to bring about the cycle that preserves man from extinction.

> . . . providence decrees that, through obstinate and desperate civil wars, they shall turn their cities into forests and the forests into dens and lairs of men. In this way, through long centuries of barbarism, rust will consume the misbegotten subtleties of malicious wits that have turned them into beasts made more inhuman by the barbarism of reflection than the first men had been made by the barbarism of sense.[22]

Thus, left to himself, despite his intelligence, man is a victim of his own self-love, and doomed to inevitable self-destruction; hence the very orderliness of history, and the preservation of mankind throughout the recurring cycles, is in itself an absolute proof of providence. The return to primitive barbarism prevents man from totally destroying himself, and this providential return, repeated time and again, cannot be the work of man. Thus 'in one of its principal aspects, this science must therefore be a rational and civil theology of divine providence.'[23]

(One is tempted to speculate that a twentieth-century Vico would amplify his argument by the claim that the destruction of the present culture and man's reduction to a simple way of life would save the world from pollution and radiation. For both us and Vico the idea of the return to the wild is morally ambiguous: it is a relapse, but also a return to certain primitive and 'pristine' virtues.)

Vico's argument is further explained by his etymological analysis of the word 'divine', which he claims comes from *divinari*, to divine in the sense of 'foresee'. It is only on account of providence that the general pattern of the future is foreseeable. Since institutions had been established by providence, 'the course of the institutions of the nations had to be, must now be, and will have to be such as our science demonstrates, even if infinite worlds were born from time to time through eternity . . . '.[24]

This is a curious but interesting argument, and it parallels one of the arguments about evolution where the very orderliness of the process taken as a whole has been held to demonstrate the work of providence. The chief difficulty with this argument, in both cases, is that the alleged working of providence is so immanent within the process that it seems hard to distinguish providence from the very laws that describe the process.[25] Hence it is not surprising that, just as Darwin convinced many that providence was superfluous in any account of human evolution, so Vico's follower, Croce, claimed that providence was superfluous in the explanation of historical evolution.

This brings us back to one of the recurring themes of this study. I have argued that providence cannot, by its very nature, be demonstrated in a straightforward, empirical way. If providence can be supported by any kind of rational reflection 'from below', that is, from reflection on human experience and on the human condition, it must be either through an attempt to interpret personal or group experience, or through an acceptance of certain metaphysical arguments. Thus in so far as history is a true science – and Vico was utterly convinced that it could be just that – it would be most odd if an historical demonstration of providence could be provided. Vico might, in principle, be able to establish

the laws of historical change, but it would be highly misleading to
call these providence, or direct evidence for providence. For
someone who believes in providence, however, they would be
examples of the means by which God steers human history. (In
principle, historians might uncover some laws that described how
man was preserved from age to age, and these laws might be both
surprising and fortunate; but to insist that they reflected the workings of an unseen God would always be going beyond the empirical
evidence. Other interpretations would always be possible.)

However, while it would be odd, for the reasons given, to look
for a proof of providence in history, it would also be odd to insist
that there is no connection between the concept of providence
and history, except for the very vague enactment of justice already
referred to, and perhaps some special involvement with Hebrew
history. I think that there is a further connection which I shall
proceed to bring out.

Both in the purely physical order and in the human order, I
have argued, any coherent account of providence demands that
there should be a certain openness which makes providential activity a possibility. Failing this we have a falsification, or at least
strong counter-evidence, for the view that providence is a factor
that makes for change in that order. Similarly, if history were
shown to be an autonomous order, totally determined by Marxist
or other laws; or on the other hand, if it were found to be a totally
meaningless recurring cycle; then there would be strong grounds
for rejecting any providential interpretation of history. The position is somewhat complicated by the logical possibility that God's
only purpose in history might be that it should be an arena in
which individual souls can be saved, and some Protestants have
appeared to see non-biblical history in this way. However, this is
a very extreme view, and most people would regard a futile human
history as counter-evidence for providence. It might still be the
case that there was providence at work in the orders of nature
and of (individual) man, but the exclusion of providence from
such an important realm as history would seem to cast doubt on
the whole concept. However, evidence for a significant direction
or progress within history would be consistent with belief in providence, and might be held to be suggestive of it.

I return therefore to the question, 'Is there evidence for either
direction or progress within non-biblical history?' There has certainly been a bewildering array of answers. To list just a few:
Kant believed in the inevitable progress of man towards the ra-

tional and the free; according to Condorcet, advancing knowledge guaranteed a Utopian future; his pupil, Comte, had a similar hope based on the role of science, but providence he regarded as irrelevant, a fiction from an earlier age. According to Hegel, history was providential, and had a glorious goal, but the 'common belief' in providence was too narrow, being concerned only with individuals and their desires and not with peoples or with the whole plan of history. Hegel held that reason, when properly understood can discern the plan in the emergence of Mind.[26] Marx took over Hegel's dialectic, but gave it a wholly materialistic interpretation, according to which history moves in an inevitable direction, determined by the underlying economic conditions, and leads eventually to a classless society. As with Vico, there is a kind of spiral return, in Marx's case from primitive communism in the cave to a true communism at the end; but unlike Vico, the return is not to be followed by a relapse, since it is the messianic final resting place of the historical process.[27] As for progress, this is not to be found in the present, for man can be more alienated under capitalism than under any previous order; but there is certainly destined to be progress following the rise of the proletariat. To mention just one more view, Reinhold Niebuhr so emphasizes the effects of original sin that he is dubious about any human progress within history, though for the faithful history is to be seen as the arena of both judgment and grace.[28] He forms a sort of opposite pole to the position of Marx, and his views recall in many ways the theme of Augustine's *City of God*.

The very variety of views representing intelligent reflection on history might be taken to suggest that there can be no demonstration of direction or progress. Nevertheless, I propose to outline an argument in favour of a certain direction in history that can reasonably be held to carry with it a limited degree of progress.

Some of the processes that have taken place in human society are probably irreversible like the change to a culture that is based on city life, and the growing emphasis on technology. Alongside both of these changes lies a still more fundamental one, namely the growing awareness of the person as being individually responsible, and as being the bearer of certain rights. This is evidenced, for example, in the near universal condemnation of collective punishment in contrast with the old view whereby children could quite properly be punished for their fathers' iniquity.[29] It is at least a plausible view that, even if man chooses, or is forced, to return to a simpler way of life in order to preserve the world's resources, this discovery[30] of the value of the individual, and also much of man's scientific and cultural complexity, will be retained. In particular, there are two aspects of this complexity that have long-term implications for moral progress, namely, the scientific enterprise itself, and modern communications.

Few people now believe the old myth that science can in every respect be ethically neutral, for there is at least the demand for integrity with respect to the scientist's own procedures and in his evaluation of the work of others. This depends on a respect for truth, sometimes at the expense of one's own cherished hopes and beliefs. Without this placing of truth above one's own good, the goals of science are simply frustrated. It can also be argued that this respect for truth, which must include the sympathetic hearing of others' views, cannot but tend to spill over into more general moral attitudes, such as respect for persons as persons. It appears that many of the leaders of the civil rights movement in the USSR have a scientific background, and this suggests that there is such a connection. Essentially, therefore, the claim is that in the very long run the demands of the scientific enterprise bring certain moral results that are progressive.

Modern communications, meanwhile, expose us to the views and situations of other people in a way that was impossible before and cannot leave us unaffected. Again, it is at least a plausible view that some of the effects of this are progressive, for communication is surely connected with the global nature of the recent upsurge in demands for human rights. It is harder to commit injustice in a corner, and increasingly oppressors feel the need to attempt a public justification for what they are doing. Just as the introduction of the jury system in ancient Athens had far-reaching results, because one had to plead one's case before a public, so it may be hoped that the very existence of a sort of international jury of public opinion will produce a long-term pressure in favour of toleration and justice. This international public opinion is clearly at an embryonic stage at present and has had only a small effect on the horrors of this decade, but the implications over the centuries are enormous.

My case here must not be misunderstood. I am certainly not claiming that scientific advance, and greater means of communication, are in themselves moral advances, only that they have implications for man that involve progress. Nor am I claiming that a world that has progressed in the ways that I envisage will necessarily be better in the sense that persons within it will be morally better. My own analysis in Chapter V implied a view in which persons can be morally better only when they voluntarily co-operate with the good, so that no environment or culture can by itself *make* better persons. But morally good persons do not exhaust the category of moral value, and a culture that contained less pain and more encouragement of moral and artistic values would be 'better' in a significant sense.

An objection to this argument might be that my standard for measuring progress is a set of human values that are purely subjective. Such an objection would be equivalent to the common charge that, when men call evolution 'progressive', they are merely imposing their own particular values on a much broader scheme of things. But regardless of what one thinks of this latter argument, the cases are not equivalent, for the second case involves contrasting men with other animals, while the first is concerned only with a human culture that is claimed to be progressive. On almost any moral system that one cares to think of, a culture that had a greater respect for the individual, for truth, for the opinions of others, and for public protest against apparent injustices, would be 'better'. If one holds a totally subjective view of ethics, this result may not be very significant; but those who seek to explore the concept of providence must also be prepared to consider that moral values may have a certain objectivity, for belief in providence and in moral objectivity tend to go together.

In concluding the argument that there is at least a plausible case for both a limited sense of direction and of progress within history, I shall mention the one fact that above all others leads me to the view that, in a significant sense, our culture is morally better than that of the Romans or of the Middle Ages, despite the horrors that persist. This is the almost complete abolition of slavery, at least in most of its forms. (Institutionalized exploitation should perhaps be regarded as the continuation of slavery in one of its forms.) When the history of slavery is fully appreciated, it may well be that someone looking back at recent centuries from the distant future will feel that the movement for its abolition, associated with Wesley, Wilberforce, and others, was the most significant movement affecting the morality of human culture since the first experiments in democracy by the Greeks. It is interesting to note that its instigators certainly believed that they were responding to the promptings of providence.

6. *The uniqueness of scripture*

In the last section we considered Vico's claim that history consists of an endless spiral of cycles. In company with most commentators I do not agree; and in disagreeing I have defended the plausibility of the view that there is both direction and progress within history. I have also disagreed with Vico's claim that history can provide a positive demonstration of providence. What, then are we to make of the remaining Vichian claim, namely, that there is a radical gulf between Hebrew and secular history?

There are two principal grounds for rejecting Vico's position on this matter, the first rational and the second religious. The first ground is that, when due allowance is made for the bias of the Old Testament writers, the vast majority of Hebrew history does look very much like the rest of history. The extraordinary persistence of the Hebrews may require an unusual explanation, but psychological explanations can at least be attempted. Freud had an ingenious one,[31] though few psychologists would now take his suggestion seriously; but there are other possibilities, for persistence is not a unique phenomenon. What we have is, rather, the most formidable example of persistence.

The religious grounds for disquiet with Vico's position is that too big a separation between biblical and non-biblical history will render much of the Bible irrelevant to us. For example, the value of the story of David is, in part at least, its very humanity, for many people can identify with his courageous but roguish character. More generally, if the Bible is held to illustrate the dealing of God with man, the events and characters must reflect events and characters as they can be now, otherwise much of the relevance is lost.

However, although I propose to reject Vico's radical separation of biblical and non-biblical history, I think that the Christian tradition cannot see biblical history quite in the same way as the rest of history. The claim that Hebrew history is different from Roman history in just the same way as Roman history is different from English or French history is inadequate. I have two reasons for this assertion.

The first reason is a somewhat subtle one, and I shall have to digress in order to explain it. Generally, there is a clear distinction between the meaning of a concept and its application in a particular situation. I am sympathetic to the view of Wittgenstein in his later writings that the meaning of a concept must be sought in

its use, and that therefore the particular application will be relevant to the meaning of the concept only in a very limited way,
since normally we already know the meaning of a concept from
hundreds of prior applications. Throughout this study, therefore,
I have sought to unwrap the concept of providence by seeing how
it is used, and how it could be used, in the contexts of nature,
man, and history. Also, and closely related to this, is the attempt
to see how the concept relates to a number of other concepts such
as God, cause, miracle, etc.

However, some concepts derive their meaning, not only from
general usage, but also from some particular, original setting, and
this fact may require a modification of Wittgenstein's insights.
Consider, for example, the concept of the 'novel'. Let us suppose
that Fielding's *Tom Jones* had been even more original than it
was, had been unlike anything before it, and yet had been followed by a whole tradition of later novels which owed their first
inspiration to *Tom Jones*. Then any account of the concept of the
novel could use hundreds of illustrations from later usage, but
when it came to describing *Tom Jones* itself, the situation would
be unusually complex, for this book would not only be an example
of a novel, it would also be formative of it. To a small extent this
is actually true of the real *Tom Jones*, for it tends to straddle the
normal distinction between the meaning of the concept of the
novel and its application.

By analogy, this illustrates the special position of the scriptures
within the Christian tradition, or of other sacred books within
other religious traditions. Here, however, there is a particular set
of books that have a special relationship to a series of concepts,
of which providence is just one. In the scriptures we find applications or illustrations of many of the key concepts used in religious language, but the meaning of these concepts is specially
related to these applications, and is in a way derived from them.
Naturally, the meaning of a concept, to a very small degree, is
derived from its use in every context, but the significance of the
biblical usage in establishing the core of meaning for concepts
such as 'God' or 'love' is of a special kind. This is part of what it
means to regard the scriptures as having some kind of authority.

Such an approach to the scriptures has as a consequence the
fact that the Bible cannot be treated by the Christian simply like
any other book. Similarly, the Hebrew history which it describes
cannot be treated exactly like any other history. It also helps to
explain why the liberal Christian can treat the Bible as 'revelation',

in one of the senses that that concept has,[32] without being committed to the view that God in some way dictated the actual words. Not only does he suggest that the writers received grace, but he can also emphasize the way in which new concepts can dawn in the minds of the readers, or concepts only dimly appreciated can become enriched, as, for example, when *eros* gives way to *agape*.

The second reason for refusing to treat biblical history exactly like other history is consequent upon the first. Although there is no need for the Christian to deny the work of providence in non-biblical history, or in the special experiences of religions outside the Judaeo-Christian tradition, the key events surrounding the Old and New Testaments must have a unique significance for him. Therefore, the history in which these events are embedded must itself be of unique importance.

It should be noted that neither of these reasons affords any ground for refusing to use the tools of ordinary historical scholarship with respect to biblical history. Rather, they both help to explain the psychological and epistemological significance of the scriptures within a tradition.

VII

The Rational Evaluation of the
Concept of Providence

1. Taking stock

I intend at this point to take stock with respect to the three fundamental issues that were raised in the introduction.

The first and most obvious issue concerned the kinds of divine activity that could be referred to. The initial analysis distinguished six kinds of activity, but only two of these were providence in the strict sense of the term. Various analogies for these two kinds of government were explored, and that which was found most helpful for general providence was that of the tide, while that which most closely reflected special providence, with its suggestion of specific decisions, was human action. There followed an exploration of how the concept of providence is used, and can be used, in the orders of nature, man, and history. Here, as in the introduction, the attempt to clarify the concept consisted partly in an analysis of how people had used the term and the distinctions they had drawn, partly in an account of the relationship of providence to other concepts, and partly in recommendations for the most helpful use of the concept.

At certain points the attempt to give a coherent account has involved a reinterpretation of providence, in particular with respect to what the Christian tradition has usually understood by the sovereignty and the omniscience of God. This reinterpretation has its roots in Aquinas' distinction between primary and secondary causality, but Aquinas was too anxious to combine his insight with traditional language about God's sovereignty.

Another way of seeing the recommendations is to consider the way in which laws are thought to operate in the orders of nature, man, and history, and while taking these laws seriously to see how it might be possible to speak of providential action, not as simply another form of law, nor as something that overrides those laws, but as a different kind of factor which can, in principle, coexist with those laws. To take the example of history, belief in providence does not involve denying that there are certain economic laws which can be used to explain and predict social movements, but it does involve rejecting Marx's belief that these laws are of an iron necessity and that they could by themselves explain all historical movements in the long run.[1]

The second issue concerns the kind of claim that is involved when religious people speak of the work of providence. The exploration of this issue contributes to the grammar of providence because here the relationship of 'providence' and of 'cause' becomes clearer. Providence, we found, could not be the object of strictly empirical, scientific investigation, and this is a conclusion reached, not as a result of being driven into a corner by the encroachment of science, but by the very grammar of the concept of providence, which 'steers' nature without overruling it. Two of the analogies that I have used to bring out this point are that of the helmsman steering his boat along a river, but not, in his capacity as helmsman, having the ability to leave the river; and that of the creative artist who is using, but at the same time is limited by, his medium. The medium constituted by the created order allows for a vast range of creative options for providence, but it also imposes limitations, so long as it is to be respected as an 'order'.

However, the discovery that a strictly empirical proof of providence is ruled out by the nature of providence does not imply that the only approach must be one of 'sheer faith' or a groundless leap into the irrational. There is an important area between scientific arguments and leaps into the dark, where it is appropriate to speak of acts of *judgment*. These occur, in particular, when men attempt to interpret and make sense of their various experiences.

The third issue is ultimately the most difficult and perplexing. Providence refers to God's activity, and yet God is said to be totally unchanged. Plato and Aristotle had illuminating accounts of how an ultimate principle could be changeless, but these accounts cannot be taken over wholesale by those who refer providence to a personal God. If it can meaningfully be said that God loves *a* and *b* and *c*, how can he not be affected? Aquinas' answer, and that of the orthodox Christian tradition, is to deny that love is an 'affection' in God, but the price of this approach is so to attenuate the analogy of love between God and man that many feel that it is no longer possible to assert that 'God is love' in any significant sense. For many sceptics, it is one more example of the erosion of the meaning of religious assertions by a series of qualifications. In contrast with the orthodox response, Whitehead and Hartshorne would prefer a break with the language of the tradition and speak of God's internal change, though only with respect to certain aspects of the Godhead, not, for example, his character or purpose. There is no doubt that many ordinary Christians have a personal faith along these lines, often not realizing that according to the mainstream theologians they have fallen into the heresy of 'patripassianism', the view that the Father can be said to suffer.

For the Christian, the problem of the relationship of the eternal God to the physical universe is centred in the question of the nature of Christ. However, it is worth re-emphasizing that the problem of how Christ is related to the Father is not the introduction of a totally new problem so much as the focussing of an ancient and inescapable problem for any theist, especially one who speaks of the love or compassion of God. For example, the Muslim has to face the question 'How can God be wholly transcendent, and yet compassionate to individual men, and communicate with them?' This is fundamentally the same question as the Jew or the Christian has to face. If it is charged that God spoke to Muhammad through Gabriel, the problem is simply put one stage further back: how did an eternal and transcendent God communicate a specific message to Gabriel? Similarly, the issue is there for every form of personal theism, and it is there because thinkers within the religious traditions of theism believe that they are trying to do justice to two aspects of their experience at the same time, namely the sense of the ultimate majesty and transcendence of God, and the experience of personal communion and grace. The problem of the nature of Christ certainly raises some extra questions, and in the section on the atonement I have tried to shed some light on these, but fundamentally these are questions *within* the larger issue that faces all theists equally. This is why I claim that the question of the nature of Christ focusses a preexisting problem. Whether this problem is to be met by a solid defence of the mainstream tradition, or by a new interpretation along the lines of Hartshorne's proposals, or in some other way,

I do not propose to pursue here, but sooner or later the thoughtful Christian must face this issue.

(Those who wish to maintain an orthodox theology, over against Whitehead and the other process philosophers, will probably point out that although God is immutable, according to the Christian tradition, it is misleading to speak as if there were no movement of any kind within God. The doctrine of the internal procession of the Son and of the Spirit, representing intelligence and will in the Godhead, and the doctrine of the external procession, manifested in creation, both indicate movement of a kind. Here, as elsewhere, a full treatment of the issues must attempt to combine the approach 'from below' with the approach 'from above'.)

2. *The options open to the rational man*

Granted that some progress has been made in examining the concept of providence, and of providing some understanding of its grammar, at least with regard to the first and second issues, it is time to approach the question of the validity of the concept. Clarity is important, but it is not everything, and faced with the momentous personal issues raised by the question of providence, it would be very odd simply to brush aside a critical evaluation and be content with only a grammatical evaluation. On the other hand, the analysis has shown that there must be some very definite limits to how far a critical evaluation can go; for example, the demand for a straightforward empirical test for providence is a demand that shows that the concept has not been understood.

In this chapter I shall argue that rational responses to the concept of providence fall into three groups, or options: the position of rejection, the position that accepts some kind of general providence only, and the position that accepts both a general and a special providence, the latter, especially, manifesting the activity of a personal God. Within each of these positions there are innumerable variations and subdivisions, but the subdivision that I shall be most concerned with arises in the case of the third option, where what I shall refer to as option 3a denies, or is agnostic about, providential change in the world of physical nature and concentrates on God's ability so to change men that they can live with physical nature as it is. Position 3b will refer to the more orthodox faith of someone within the mainstream tradition.

It may seem strange that I should allow that there can be such a variety of 'rational' positions. I certainly do not mean to imply that all positions taken by people on religion are rational, far from it. In the context of the choices that face us at this point I am using the word 'rational' in a particular and rather narrow sense. By a rational position I mean one that is capable of satisfying two basic criteria, first, internal consistency, and second, consistency with the most obvious facts of experience. One could describe this as a demand for both 'internal' and 'external' coherence. Unfortunately, even this usage of 'rational' is not without its difficulties, for there will always be disputes about borderline cases with respect to both internal and external coherence. Moreover, the concept of the 'rational' is a loaded one, with a certain cultural relativity. For example, Europeans tend to regard their educational system, or form of government, as 'rational', while those of other parts of the world are held to be less so. Further, one might ask, 'What exactly are the facts of religious experience and of the world which any rational philosophy must take account of?'

Despite the obvious difficulties, there is a sense in which we can often make an important distinction between rational and irrational positions, applying the two criteria that I have proposed. For example, to say that the moon is full of cheese has always been irrational. However, to say that it is full of water is false, although two hundred years ago it would not have been irrational had the suggestion been backed up by some kind of argument that did not contradict the facts as then known. This brings out the cultural relativity of the rational. Today it would be irrational for someone to hold that the moon is full of water, for there is a kind of consensus about what is an open and what is a closed matter, similar to the kind of scientific consensus of which Polanyi writes.[2] This consensus is certainly not infallible, and thus it is most important not to confuse the categories of the true and of the rational. When I claim that a position is rational I mean that it is plausible, that it might be true, and that it is not manifestly contradictory in either of the two ways that I have indicated.

Strictly speaking, many aspects of religion are neither rational nor irrational, but rather 'non-rational'. It is misleading to ask whether they are consistent, when 'consistent' is used in the context of 'consistent with' something else. The experiences that we call religious are in themselves just *experiences* of certain kinds, they are simply non-rational. In a similar way we need the categories of the non-moral and the non-logical in order to avoid having to put things into unsuitable categories. However, in the philosophy of religion we are frequently attempting to make judgments about these non-rational experiences, and then criteria of consistency arise.

Given this limited use of the 'rational', it should not be surprising that a large number of different positions can be dignified by this title. Whenever we are not in a position to know the truth, there may be many possible positions that might be true, in addition to many that could not possibly be true. Moreover, very few religious people claim to have *knowledge* of the divine order; otherwise the word 'faith' would not be appropriate, as Paul intimated.[3] Further still, intelligent reflection on religion must include an attempt to interpret one's own experiences, and different people have had very different experiences. Hence it is not surprising if rational men take up different positions with regard to religion. As we saw in the introduction, it may be rational for one man to believe something that it would be irrational for another to believe, given their different experiences.

The attempt to use judgment in interpreting one's personal experience of life is indeed the most important of the rational elements in the evaluation of religion. There is the vital experiential element, plus an act of judgment that accepts one interpretation as more convincing than others on grounds of coherence. But this judgment is made in a very complex context. In addition to one's judgment about a particular experience there is the evaluation of the internal coherence and intelligibility of an overall position, one's decision about whether the world in general is compatible with religious claims, one's judgment of the consistency and adequacy of other world views, one's evaluation and interpretation of the experience of other people, and so on. Alongside these acts of judgment it may be that some evaluation of the traditional metaphysical arguments is also called for; otherwise it might be claimed that one cannot have a reason for interpreting one's experience with reference to an alleged metaphysical reality, such as God.

Many of these acts of judgment are essentially negative. Rather than proving that x is the case, they show that x might be the case, or that y and z are not the case. This is a feature of much recent apologetics, which, in contrast with Aquinas' classical proofs for the existence of God, provide a kind of negative natural theology, whereby it is alleged that none of the objections, like that based on the problem of evil, disprove Christianity, and that various suggested alternatives are all unsatisfactory. However, the contrast between a positive and a negative approach is not as clear-cut as it might seem. If a certain position remains coherent and possible after multiple attacks, and if at the same time all the alternatives that one considers seem fragile, then some kind of positive pressure in favour of the initial position begins to be built up. It is rather like drawing straws until only one is left, and then one is forced to take that one. This is not a perfect analogy, because one could never prove that there were not other possible positions that one had not thought of, which might be even more coherent. Nevertheless, it remains true that someone following a purely negative course might end up making a rational judgment in favour of the one position that continued to stand up to criticism.

On several occasions I have noted that a phenomenon, like, for example, the complexity of evolution, while not direct evidence for providence, is suggestive of it for many people. This fact should be linked with the point of the last paragraph. There can be a cumulative effect of many suggestive factors which can quite properly improve or weaken the plausibility of a world view.

3. Option one, the rejection of providence

I might have called this first option the agnostic approach, but this would have been misleading. In the first place Christians, strictly speaking, are 'agnostics', for they claim to believe, not to know.[4] (Colloquially, of course, the term is used to refer to those who neither know nor believe.) Further, within this position I want to include many whose rejection of providence would be put much more forcibly than it would by the typical agnostic.

Some of those who would advocate a forceful rejection of providence would be those positivists who claim, not that religious assertions are false, but that they are literally meaningless. For such it would not be enough to show that the concept of providence had a certain grammar (though the early positivists did not seem to be sufficiently aware of the significance of this grammar), for providence is alleged to be the activity of God, and the concept of God is held by them to be so vague that it cannot have anything other than emotive meaning. Supporters of this view will probably be suspicious of my claim that a falsification of providence, or strong counter-evidence, could in principle be provided by the investigation of nature or man or history. They would want to know more precisely what these orders would have to be like in order to constitute counter-evidence.

It is important to see that a positivist who raises issues such as this does not need to deny the reality of religious experiences, like that of the numinous. As R. W. Hepburn and others have pointed out, the existence of a particular kind of experience is one thing, its interpretation another. Some of those who are well informed about the nature of many kinds of religious experience would consistently reject interpretations that brought in the concept of God.[5]

Somewhat paradoxically, the atheistic group, who would also strongly reject providential interpretations of experience, would tend to do so precisely because they think that the orders of nature, man, and history, as now constituted, do provide a falsification of the claim that a God is active. The world is too closed a system, or man too wretched and miserable, or history too much a saga of woe, for providential interpretations to be believable. Thus, for them, the concept of providence is significant but false, in the sense that there is no reality corresponding to the concept. While positivism is rare, except in academic circles, this latter position is very common among intelligent people, and it is often reached, after an initial period of belief, as a result of some tragic experience. The emphasis that I have brought out, on a providence that respects the autonomy of the orders, and the denial that a great deal of what happens can in any helpful way be called 'God's will', shows, in my view, that many of these rejections are based on a false notion of the concept of providence. However, I do not wish to claim that a more adequate understanding of providence would result in the conversion of large numbers of atheists. While it takes much force from the atheist camp, in that it is harder to show that human misery conflicts with belief in providence, by the same token it may be held to add much force to the positivist camp, for both verification and falsification become harder to substantiate. The less that religious claims are thought to support expected changes in the ordinary world, or to resemble scientific or practical claims, the more some people will regard them as unworthy of serious consideration. Also, many who might be persuaded by a more adequate account of the meaning of providence to leave the atheist camp, on the grounds that experience did not, after all, disprove providential interpretations, would settle in the agnostic camp, in the colloquial sense of that term.

Another group will forcefully reject the concept of providence because of some alternative world view which rules it out. The most important current example of this is Marxism, for which religion and religious assertions, while having a certain kind of meaning, are nevertheless examples of a 'false consciousness'.

4. *Option two, belief in an impersonal spiritual principle*

My treatment of options two and three is longer than my treatment of option one, but this does not reflect an *a priori* assumption that they are more rational. The principal aim of this book is to understand the concept of providence, and we are clearly likely to learn more about its meaning from those who use it than from those who do not. This explains the otherwise disproportionate treatment of options two and three.

Option two embraces as many different views as option one. They have in common the belief that the order displayed in the universe, and the nature of change within it, either demands or suggests something more in the way of explanation than the properties of the physical order itself, and that a spiritual principle of some kind, that may or may not be called God, is operative. However, there is no belief in a personal God, who can have knowledge of, or relationship to, individual persons. Also there is no belief that the universe is either 'steered' or governed by anything corresponding to an agent that can make decisions or have acts of will. Change is the result of permanent and relentless forces, but some of these are spiritual.

In the foregoing paragraph I have used the word 'spiritual' twice. This is a term which holders of option one will have great difficulty with. They will certainly approve the rejection of an anthropomorphic deity, but they may not be much happier about the replacement. Unfortunately, one cannot give a quick definition of 'spiritual', any more than one can give a quick definition of providence, because the meaning of these terms arises in the context of traditions that use them, and I have argued that there is no short cut that avoids the arduous task of trying to understand a tradition in order to unravel the grammar of a concept within it. However, a little can be said by way of an initial clarification. The concept of the spiritual is a broader one than the concept of God and is common to a large number of religions, some of which do not believe in a special providence or a personal God. The central idea is of an *invisible* principle, or entity, or force, perhaps originally conceived animistically. This principle is always something important; often it is what ought to be most valued, sometimes it is dangerous. Often it suggests something free and unpredictable. The gods are spirits, and so, usually, are the invisible and central aspects of persons. Spiritual principles and forces are those that work unseen but are nevertheless in some way ultimate; for the visible order is linked with, and depends on, an unseen order.

Despite the difficulty in giving an adequate characterization of spiritual principles, we must recognize that they are central to the beliefs of many intelligent and thoughful men, including many who hold to non-theistic religions. Moreover, belief in such principles, when these affect nature, or man, or history, can be described as belief in a general providence, provided that we remember that this expression is not necessarily used, and that unlike the belief of those who take option three, belief in a general providence does not have to reflect the providence of a personal God. Thus, spiritual forces, like general providence, work in a way that is illustrated by the analogy of the tide, and as we have seen, this allows us to include many dramatic and spectacular events under the sway of general providence, without the introduction of a personal God. They are analogous to tidal bores.

I shall proceed to describe two main varieties of this option and then to indicate the kinds of rational grounds that are common to them.

The seventeenth- and eighteenth-century deists afford one interesting example of this option. Here the tendency is to exalt the role of reason in religion and to depreciate that of miracle, revelation, and prophecy. The ablest writer in the original group was probably Tindal, and it is worth noting that his starting point was not so much the claims of reason, as the implications, as he saw them, of the changelessness of God. From this changelessness there followed, so he argued, the necessity that all men should be treated alike. Therefore, men are drawn to the truth not by special revelations, but by what is equally revealed to all men in nature, and by the moral law that is the property of all.[6] From men like Tindal there developed during the eighteenth century a popular deism in which God was seen as the great clockmaker, whose influence in the present is primarily or exclusively to be found in the laws laid down in the original construction of the clock. There is a strong emphasis on what I have referred to as 'natural' rewards and punishments that are consequent upon our response to the moral law, and it is through these that providence is operative in the present.

The term 'deist' is now rare, and almost always used with a backward reference to men such as Herbert of Cherbury, Toland, and Tindal, but a position that is essentially similar is common in the West. There are large numbers of people who cannot believe in the personal God of orthodox Christianity or Judaism or Islam, but who still consider themselves to have a religion. Sometimes they will talk about God in an impersonal way, sometimes of spiritual principles, and often there will be a confused blend of Western and Eastern ideas. This sounds disparaging, but I do not mean it to be so. Modern man is trying to adjust to a rapidly changing intellectual climate, with a sudden exposure to many ideas that are basically foreign to the traditional culture of the West, and it is not surprising if the interim positions of many searchers after truth look like a jumble of borrowings from many different places. (Primitive Christianity probably looked like this to the intelligent pagan.)

Among the resting places for these seekers, especially those who have some real familiarity with Eastern ideas, are various forms of monism, the other principle variant of option two. I have previously referred to the perennial attraction of monistic views during the discussion of the analogy between change in space and change in time. If all things are ultimately one and partake of the one spiritual principle that animates all being, then change is ultimately an illusion, and the problem of relating a changeless God to a changing world begins to evaporate. It only seems a problem so long as we are under the spell or the illusion of the apparently multiple and changing order. However, within such a view there can be a strong emphasis on a principle corresponding to general providence. The human mind, which at present tends to exhibit a certain false individuality, is drawn towards an ultimate unity with the One, a reality that is already there at the centre of each person. For Plotinus, perhaps the greatest of the Western monists, building on Plato's *Symposium*, what draws all men to their inner centre, where they can become united with the One, is the vision of beauty.[7] Plotinus also gives us, in his third *Ennead*, an eloquent account of providence from the point of view of one who denies that there is a personal God. Perhaps more familiar today are some of the great monistic systems of the East, notably that of Sankara,[8] and of some traditions within Buddhism.

The grounds put forward to support positions of this kind are legion, though they are often not forcibly expressed in front of the ordinary man, since few deists or monists have anything corresponding to missionary zeal. Indeed there is something incongruous in someone who holds such views being over-worried about whether others share them. I think that it would be fair to observe, however, that the principle ground, if expressed, is simply the view that the over all philosophy is adequate, and in the case of monism that it provides a consistent interpretation of life, especially if one takes into account mystical experience. Also it provides a philosophy to live by. Over against position one there might well be the claim that a monistic philosophy deals with the whole of man's experience while position one does not. Over against position three there might well be the claim that this second position has a certain advantage of economy and is more in accord with Occam's principle, 'Do not multiply entities needlessly'. Monism appears to have a basic simplicity whose attraction is felt by many, even among those who ultimately reject it.

Monists tend to regard the particular beliefs of option three, including belief in a personal God, with a certain tolerance. Such beliefs are not actually correct, but they can represent a sort of 'lower knowledge' which may be appropriate and helpful for those not yet ready for the 'higher knowledge' of ultimate reality that is properly expressed only in a monistic philosophy.

Before leaving option two I want to express an attitude to the religious life which is typical of this option, and which amounts to a kind of argument for it. According to the ordinary theist, opportunities are meant to be used as they occur, and then, having been used, they tend to be regarded as providential. For example, I may miss an aeroplane, and while waiting for the next one several new opportunities inevitably present themselves. This might be the occasion for training in patience, or for meeting the person whom I am going to marry, or for having some other formative experience. The religious person who has developed the attitude of using such occasions creatively will very likely find that some significant event occurs and will then give thanks to God for his special providence. However, someone who believes only in a general providence might well comment: 'But you find opportunities whatever happens; so how can you properly thank a special providence for providing *this* opportunity, as if it had been contrived? If you had caught the plane you would now be thanking God for some other opportunity. What this example illustrates is not the work of a special providence, but the permanent spiritual challenge to respond to opportunities, and the reality of the opportunities that are made possible by the spiritual laws that surround us. The spiritual experience is real, but it does not demonstrate the need for a personal God; it can be explained more economically without such a deity.'

5. *Option three, providence as the activity of a personal God*

The three options that I am describing are not like water-tight compartments, for some people would not wish to be placed firmly within any of the three, but within one of the many intermediate positions that are possible. Nevertheless, the options represent crucial divisions within the philosophy of religion and indicate issues that require a rational judgment. Moreover, those who hold to an orthodox variation of Christianity or Judaism or Islam are bound to place themselves within the range of option three, for here the emphasis is on a personal God as revealed in the Old and New Testaments and in the Koran. This, in turn, so I have argued, commits those within these religions either to a belief in special providence, or miracle, or both; for otherwise it is hard to see what grounds there can be for believing that God is personal, or what meaning the claim that he is personal can have. Most, but not all, of those who come within the range of option three, would also be content to accept the working of a general providence.

It is important to see that an assessment of the validity of the concept of providence within option three is tied up with an exposition of *what* is held to be the case. Restricting myself to the issue as it faces the Christian, it will not do to make an absolute contrast between the questions 'What is Christianity?' and 'What are the grounds for believing in Christianity?' This is particularly evident if one is asking how far a belief is 'rational', in the sense of that term that I have adopted; for the very description of what the Christian faith consists of will be vital to the determination of whether it is internally and externally coherent. There is always the further question, 'Are the claims made by this religion actually true?', except for those who deny that religious assertions are truth claims at all. Thus I am not committing myself to a pure coherence theory of truth. However, it is doubtful whether the philosopher, as philosopher, is likely to be able finally to resolve this question, any more than the historian, as historian, is likely finally to settle the question of the resurrection. This is why the apologetics that is in principle possible now is very different from the apologetics represented by the classical proofs for the existence of God. Philosophy is highly relevant for the rational assessment of the validity of religious positions, but its chief role is to clarify the assertions, and then to assess the internal and external coherence as far as it can. If, when this has been done, a position appears rational in the sense referred to, the question of the actual truth of the position must be decided by each person for himself. This decision is not, of course, simply a matter of reasoning, for faith involves more than acts of judgment. Nevertheless, acts of judgment can be involved, and I suspect ought to be involved, especially as each person ponders the proper interpretation of his own experience.

Since clarification is so important for the rational assessment of a position, and since option three centres on belief in a personal God, can one say more clearly what the Christian tradition means by 'personal', beyond the emphasis that has already been made, namely that it refers to God's knowledge of and relationship with individual persons? In answer we can at least summarize a fairly representative view within the mainstream tradition. Just as there is an analogy between the providence of man, as a species of prudence, and the providence of God, so there is an analogy between the person we encounter in human relationships, and the personal nature of God. There is a certain anthropomorphism in this. However, if man is made in the image of God, then this is not 'sheer anthropomorphism', that is, a totally unjustified magnification of man which is then termed God. It is the application of the best analogy available, and of one that has in an important sense been 'given' to us. Moreover, religious experience suggests that God is more like a person than a thing, because we associate with 'person' such concepts as awareness, activity, self-direction, purpose, response to values, all of which we ascribe to God. However, we have seen that all words that describe God analogically must regard him as the prime analogue, that is, if they are words such as good, wise, holy, etc. that can be applied strictly to God.[9] Thus although we first learn the concept of person, as we learn the concept of father, from human experience, nevertheless the concept properly belongs in its fullest sense only to God.

This last point not only warns Christians about the danger of building God in their own image in the wrong way; it also has a most important consequence for our concept of person as we apply it to human beings. We have to relearn the meaning of our own personal nature through our encounter with God, since it is only he that is fully personal. This is in accord with several themes in this study; for example, in the case of the atonement theory, an adequate understanding of the primitive Christian experience demands the discovery of what it meant to be 'in Christ', namely, an extraordinary heightening of experience in which individuality was transformed. Moreover, if relationship is in part constitutive of the person, becoming full persons involves, according to the New Testament way of seeing things, an extension of relationships that has as its precondition a dying to the 'old man' and being 'born again'.[10] Another consequence of having to relearn the nature of personhood can be a new respect for the integrity of each potential person, congruous with the respect that God shows for the integrity of the orders of nature, man, and history, and in particular the respect he shows for the individual human being. For example, there is a link between our understanding of the manner in which grace works and the insights we already have concerning the way to treat those in need. Our purpose is not simply to alleviate the suffering, but to help the person to achieve a certain independence. We want to end up as friends, not as benefactors.[11]

Since reason can at best show the coherence of the Christian position, not its truth, and since the actual acceptance of it must be in part an act of faith, it follows that option three has a curious relationship with options one and two. Although it may seem paradoxical, it requires, for faith to be possible, that at least one of them can be seriously entertained. Faith has to involve an existential commitment, and consequently a certain risk, even though it holds that what it believes is in fact the truth. Thus it must be the case, if there is to be a meaningful act of faith, that God is not so immediately revealed that there is no need of a voluntary response, and in particular a response that depends upon love. Faith must take place in a context in which it is possible *not* to respond; otherwise a whole dimension of personal experience, vital for our growth as persons, is lacking. The ancient *dictum*, *fides quaerens intellectum*, means not only that faith is seeking an understanding that it does not yet possess, but that from a purely rational point of view it must be faced with at least one other option. There are also many non-options, that is, basically untenable positions which it would be irrational and, for those who know this to be so, also immoral to adopt; but this, too, may be a part of the required context for an adequate faith. The man who seeks a faith to live by is also a rational animal who must seek a faith he can believe in with intellectual integrity. In

Platonic language, God is not only the good we respond to, and the beauty we are drawn to; he is also the truth we seek to discover.

It would be very easy to misrepresent the position that I have just defended. One misrepresentation would be to see it merely as special pleading of the following kind. 'We can't prove the truth of Christianity, so let's make a virtue out of necessity, and make the very fact that it can't be proved an argument in its favour!' Against this suggestion it should be pointed out that it is absurd to treat faith in God like belief in, say, a planet beyond Pluto's orbit. Faith must have a personal dimension. Also, the claim that the nature of faith demands a certain risk is not in itself an argument in favour of the truth of the Christian position; it is a clue to understanding what kinds of argument there could be for positions of this kind. Philosophically, I am trying to show that Christianity is possible, not that it is true; but in order to show that it is possible I have to make clearer what it is, and this includes a clarification of the nature of faith.

Another misrepresentation is to see faith as something akin to Pascal's wager. 'There's all to gain, and nothing to lose by faith, so let us believe.'[12] Although Pascal was himself a man of profound faith, this suggestion is clearly not a description of the faith I describe, which is both a belief that a certain position is true, and a personal response. The wager, strictly speaking, is neither.

Yet another misrepresentation is the description of faith as the *will* to believe. The position of William James, the main supporter of this view,[13] has some similarities with my own, for he too discusses options, or what he calls 'living options', which the rational man can accept with integrity. He certainly does not suggest that one can properly will to believe anything, but he does think that an act of will can be the decisive factor, and the proper factor, in choosing between these living options. However, this position too does not take seriously enough the nature of faith as a personal response.

There is, however, a substantial objection to the nature of faith as I have described it in the foregoing discussion, namely, that it is still too intellectualist. I have written of faith as if it were the acceptance of the truth of a set of possible claims, whereas my own emphasis on the personal dimension essential to faith might suggest that it is not like this at all, but more like a simple trust in God or in Jesus. After all, it might be pointed out, the first Christian creed was not a string of formulas about the nature of

God and of the universe, but a simple affirmation, 'Christ is Lord'.[14]

I do not intend to belittle the faith of the simple man, nor that of the agnostic who has simply decided to try and follow the 'way' of Christ, even though he cannot honestly say that he believes any of the traditional claims made about Jesus. Nevertheless, for any intelligent Christian there must be a search for some *philosophy* of life. In other words, the typical religious seeker is not only looking for a personal leader, although this may be an important element in his religion; he is looking for a world view that will satisfy his searching at several levels, personal, emotional, and intellectual. Without this integrated search by the whole person, there is the danger of a purely arbitrary attachment to some charismatic leader, an attachment that has led to forms of fanaticism that are demonic, even if the leader is nominally 'Christ'. Further, as I stressed in Chapter II, Christianity could never have spread very far if it had not attempted to meet the challenge of the Greek philosophy of its early years, for this represented the intellectual curiosity of man as such. If Christ is in any significant sense 'the word of truth'[15], and if Christians are to attempt to accept Peter's call to give *reasons* for their hope,[16] then for the typical Christian some philosophy is implicit in his belief; and if he is an intelligent and educated Christian his own integrity will force him to make this philosophy as coherent and intelligible as possible. However, if it is a Christian philosophy he seeks, it will not be one that expects to eliminate all mystery, or be able to comprehend all reality within a complete system. He will have stronger grounds even than the empiricists for stressing the limitations of our knowledge.

The fact that there are some seekers who feel able to say 'Christ is Lord', but who cannot as yet embrace anything corresponding to a Christian philosophy, will serve to introduce the varieties of view comprehended under option three. Those who, amidst a sea of doubt, cling to an existential commitment to try and follow the example of Jesus, and who repeat this first creed with sincerity, are, in my view, Christians, in a legitimate sense of the term, even though they cannot yet be said to have a Christian philosophy. Not far removed from them are those whom I shall describe as holding option 3a. Here I am thinking of Bultmann and of all those who believe in the power of God, through grace, to assist in personal change. However, they do not expect God to change the world except through themselves, and they may even deny

that God *can* change the world directly. The truth of Christianity
is manifested through the saints who are able to accept the world,
to live with suffering, and where possible, to share it, alleviate it,
and transform it.

A powerful and interesting exponent of option 3a is Bonhoeffer.
He contrasted 'Christianity', as he saw it, with what most people
mean by 'religion', precisely because he did not believe that God
was active in the world except in 'weakness', though this was a
kind of weakness that was ultimately decisive so long as we are
concerned with human change. Writing from the prison where he
was eventually executed by the Nazis he says, 'God lets himself
be pushed out of the world on to the cross. He is weak and
powerless in the world, and that is precisely the way, the only
way, in which he is with us and helps us'. A little earlier he says,
'God as a working hypothesis in morals, politics, or science has
been surmounted and abolished; and the same thing has happened
in philosophy and religion,' and he concludes that we must live in
the world '*etsi deus non daretur*', (as if there were no God).[17]

Bonhoeffer's powerful style tends to mislead the reader into
thinking that he is even more removed from orthodox Christianity
than he actually is. Although he does want to make a sharp break
with many traditional beliefs, he does most strongly believe that
a personal God gives inner and personal strength to the believer.[18]
Thus there is a place for special providence within his world view,
though quite often he writes as if there were not.

In contrast with option 3a is that of 3b, which represents the
mainstream Christian tradition. Under this subdivision there are
again a large number of positions represented, including the world
views of many of the Christians who consider themselves (Greek
or Russian) Orthodox, Roman Catholic, or Protestant. What they
have in common is the belief that special providence works not
only at the purely human level, but also at the level of physical
nature and of history. At least one reason for this belief may well
be a suspicion of the dualism involved in positions like those of
Bultmann. More generally, however, they consider that there is
no philosophical need to restrict God's action in the way that
Bultmann does, and that the experiential evidence of Christians
supports a more thorough-going involvement of God in the
changes of nature, man, and history.

The contrast between options 3a and 3b can be illustrated by
their different attitudes to the resurrection. Bultmann, and those
like him, are not concerned with the resurrection as a physical

event within human history, but it is nevertheless of crucial importance for them. It is a way of describing or of focussing for us the transforming power of God, for the Christian experiences a new and 'risen' life when he receives God's grace. The resurrection, therefore, stands for a kind of truth, but not for an historical event. For the mainstream tradition the symbolic meaning of the resurrection is also important, but it is held to be expressed through an actual event. Here, and in the traditional account of the incarnation by which 'the word became flesh', there is an inescapable relationship of God to the created order that cannot, on this view, be confined to a limited dimension, that of persons. For option 3b the resurrection is a miracle, not strictly speaking an example of special providence; but it is the crowning example of God's involvement in the three orders, an involvement normally manifested to the believer in acts of providence.

Under option 3b I do not wish to embrace all the views maintained by Christians who reject option 3a, or who call themselves orthodox. I am concerned in this chapter with *rational* options, in the sense described; and although I do hold that there can be Christian philosophies of both types 3a and 3b that can be rational, this does not entail that the over all philosophies of all, or even most Christians, are rational. (Nor, on the other hand, do I think that most non-Christian philosophies are rational either. What I have maintained is that there is a variety of possible rational positions, and that these can be placed in three main groups.) The irrationality may be a pervasive one, that runs through the whole outlook, or it may be a more modest one, in that some particular beliefs are irrational, whereas the general scheme is rational.

A good example of a particular irrational belief is the view that human beings can be born in a state of guilt. As I have indicated, many recent theologians have tried to reinterpret the doctrine of original sin in order to avoid this belief. Another example is the belief of many fundamentalists[19] that Adam, as an historical person, was created in a moment of time. Logically it might be possible suddenly to create an embryo, and perhaps a baby, but a 'man', who must have a moral character if he is to be a human person in a significant sense, and who must therefore have a *history* in which he has participated, *could not* be made except through an historical process. God could no more achieve an instant Adam than a square circle.

The claim that many but not all Christian philosophies are irrational brings us back to the question of paradoxes within the philosophy of religion.[20] Holders of option one will probably claim that all Christian philosophies are inevitably irrational because of their inclusion of paradoxes, but in response the Christian philosopher must stress a crucial distinction. In origin the word 'paradox' simply means 'contrary to received opinion'. In this elementary sense of the term most, if not all philosophies, include paradoxes. More colloquially, the term tends to mean either 'self-contradictory' or 'apparently self-contradictory'. However, there is a vast difference between these two renderings. As I pointed out in the introduction, scientists and others have no choice but to use paradoxes of this second kind, for very often our partial view of reality entails that things *appear* contradictory. For example, a cylinder in a box may look rectangular from a hole on top of the box, and circular from a hole at one end; but the two claims, 'It's circular' and 'It's rectangular', are only apparently contradictory, since the paradox is resolved when a broader view is taken that comprehends three dimensions.

Paradox is certainly unavoidable in all religious philosophies. The Christian should argue that his paradoxes are like those of the apprently different shapes in the box with the added complication that from the human level there can be no final resolution of many of his paradoxes, at least not on this level of existence. If this suggestion is objected to in principle, one has only to point to the fact that contemporary physics is amassing new paradoxes of this kind within its own discipline.

It follows that the presence of paradox does not by itself entail that a philosophy is irrational. There is irrationality only if (*a*) it is claimed that the paradox is ultimate, and not simply the result of our inadequate grasp of reality, or (*b*) there are no good grounds, rooted in experience, for asserting the two alleged truths that appear to conflict. Thus it can be maintained that many but not all Christian philosophies are irrational. However, what tends to happen is that people use the excuse of the possibility of legitimate paradox to hold positions that experience does not in fact warrant. In particular, I am thinking of the claim that whatever happens is an expression of God's will, and yet at the same time that there is a significant human freedom, so that we can be held accountable for our deeds. *The Westminster Confession*, for example, holds to both of these alleged truths, but asserts that they do not conflict from God's point of view.[21] But there is dangerous reasoning here. There is a glaring paradox between the view that God is the cause of every tiny movement and the view that man is responsible. While it is necessary for an adequate Christian philosophy to hold to a belief in freedom, it is not required by this same philosophy that God be in control of every event in the way in which Calvin and the *Confession* claim. Nor is this deterministic claim suggested by human experience. This, therefore, is a view that must be abandoned by the Christian who seeks a rational philosophy, and therefore I have claimed that the Christian account of God's sovereignty and omniscience must be reinterpreted.

6. An argument for special providence

Having discussed what kind of position is involved in option three it remains to summarize the kind of rational defence that is appropriate to it.

It should be clear that the traditional metaphysical arguments for the existence of God, even if accepted as valid, cannot be sufficient for the defence of option three, since they do not conclude with a God that must be seen as personal. There has been a tendency to jump from the 'God' allegedly demonstrated by the cosmological or teleological arguments to the 'God' of the New Testament. Aquinas, for example, concluded his argument from motion, 'Hence one is bound to arrive at some first cause of change not itself being changed by anything, and this is what everybody understands by God.'[22] But this is not what everybody understands by God, for Aristotle, who used essentially the same argument, meant by 'God' something very different from the personal God of Christianity. Moreover, since all the metaphysical arguments are concerned with the ground of the universe as a whole, or with change in general, there is no necessity for the source to be other than what is adequate for this overall existence or overall change.

The kinds of rational defence that are appropriate should be clear from the previous analysis. They include an attempt to state *what* the Christian philosophy is in a way that makes it internally and externally coherent. They include a negative natural theology in which alternative possibilities are reviewed, and the objections to the Christian philosophy are weighed. For the contemporary Christian the defence must also include an account of the different kinds of falsification of religious claims that are possible in principle, and which therefore indicate that belief in providence is not compatible with any state of affairs whatsoever. This is necessary in order to support the claim that a meaningful *assertion* is being made when providence is held to be at work. Altogether I have indicated six kinds of falsification of providence claims that are theoretically possible.[23] After all of this we begin to approach the area of personal judgment, where philosophy, as a public investigation of meaning and truth, has to give way to the individual's attempt to interpret his own experience. In this field there soon comes a point where the outsider can only be silent. He may express dismay and suspicion about the other's alleged experiences and about his interpretation of them, but since no one can enter another person's mind, some decisions are ultimately private, even though they may involve judgment.

However, there is one further kind of argument that is relevant to the evaluation of option three, and I shall present it as a modification of Kant's moral argument. Like Kant, I shall argue that it is not to be confused with the traditional metaphysical arguments. Further, I shall argue that it is appropriate for belief in a being who has to be grasped, if at all, by faith. A similar argument is hinted at in the writings of T. S. Eliot.[24]

In his *Critique of Practical Reason* Kant argues that for morality to be possible there are certain preconditions, namely freedom, immortality, and God. Without these 'postulates', required by the practical reason of every man, there could be no significant morality, among other reasons because morality would be demanding what it was impossible to achieve.[25] The argument that I propose to develop is different from Kant's, in that I am not going to argue that belief in personal immortality is essential as a precondition for a significant morality. I agree with Hepburn on this point.[26] But it is similar in that I shall argue that belief in a personal God is a precondition if love is to have the status that many men, and certainly all Christians, find themselves compelled to give it. Thus the argument is not that there must be a personal God, either in consequence of *a priori* logic or of some *a posteriori* argument from sensory experience; but that, *if* love is to have the significance which many attach to it, then a precondition of its having this significance is that it is grounded in a loving God.

Once again we have a problem of meaning. The concept of love, like so many other concepts, is in need of analysis. Fortunately, however, far more people are aware of the basic grammar of the Christian concept of love, *agape*, than are aware of the grammar of providence. Despite the obviously debased use of the word in many instances, many people are perfectly aware that such usage, including sometimes their own, is debased, precisely because they have some familiarity with the New Testament use of love. Also they may be familiar with the concept through its use in other traditions, like that of recent humanism, which, by its own admission, is deeply influenced by the ethical teaching of Jesus. As I have shown, the New Testament is both illustrative of, and in its central theme in part constitutive of, the concept of love. Many people who reject what they regard as unnecessary metaphysical elements in the text are nevertheless deeply committed to this concept of love, a concept that is held by them to have ultimate ethical significance.

But now comes an awkward question. Is this concept of love, when accepted as central for morality, central merely because we feel it to be so, as a result of our environment and other conditioning factors? Or is it central because it is, as a matter of truth, actually central through its own intrinsic quality? On the first view, the explanation for the central role of love is basically psychological. On the second view, love is central because it reflects some basic truth about the universe, for at the heart of the universe there *is* personal love. However, if one opts for the first view, which probably corresponds to the philosophy of most contemporary Westerners who have asked themselves this kind of question, can one both accept love as that ideal of the moral life that makes *categorical* demands on all men, and at the same time believe that its status depends on one's psychological conditioning? This seems to involve a contradiction; for only if love is believed to reflect what *is* a supreme value in the universe can the reasonable man believe that it has a *categorical and unconditional* force.

An analogy can be found for this problem in the difficulty of having an *unconditional* loyalty to a human leader, unless one really believes that the leader has a legitimate authority that is total. Once one begins to doubt the status of the leader, it is difficult to see how one's loyalty can in fact be unconditional, even though one might pay lip service to the total demands made by the leader. The unconditional demand to love is, of course, very different from the unconditional demand to obey an individual, even to obey Jesus of Nazareth[27], because the very nature of love involves a respect for persons that would be contradicted by blind obedience to orders, even if they happened to correspond exactly with what is good. However, the analogy holds in so far as regarding the ideal of love as unconditional depends on believing it to have an ultimate status; it cannot have an ultimate status if one holds a relativistic philosophy in terms of which love does not reflect an objective truth. However, if the ultimate ground of the universe is love, and if the source of all life can better be described by the name of 'love' than by any other, and if man is made to respond to this love, and if he can discover his fulfilment in this response of love, then there is a complete congruity or harmony between man's ideal and reality itself. Man then has a philosophy that is adequate for the vastness of the moral ideal that he sees before him.

This is not a 'proof' for the reality of God. It is a claim that an implication of the moral stand that many people have *already* committed themselves to is a personal God. Only if love is grounded in such a being can it be adequate as a moral ideal.

For someone who has a personal commitment to love, this argument, I believe, has much force. Moreover, it is perfectly compatible with the realization that a response to God must be one of faith. The argument is essentially one of drawing out the implications of what is already a response to God. Within the Christian tradition any genuine personal response to love is already a response to God, even if the one who loves does not realize this. The 'word' is revealed to every man as he comes across the good, the true, and the beautiful, and any positive response to any of these must be, however unknowingly, a response to God.

For one who accepts the unconditional nature of the demand to love, this argument would not, of course, necessarily imply the truth of Christianity, for belief in a personal ground of the universe is also found in Judaism and Islam, and also in some versions of Buddhism and Hinduism, etc. Whether one can argue for the truth of some more particular system is another matter. Some would claim that at the heart of all these religions there is a common core, some would claim that their experience, and the demands of coherence, indicate that one version of personal theism is more adequate than others, or more appropriate as an account of the ultimate source of love. This is a question that I shall not pursue here.

Notes

Chapter I Introduction

1. I am not here contrasting Western Christianity with Eastern Christianity, but Christianity in general, which is mostly a Western phenomenon, with Eastern thought.
2. *Erewhon*, chapter 4.
3. D. W. Prowse, *Cornhill Magazine*, London, April 1904, p. 541.
4. Quoted in G. G. Coulton, *Mediaeval Panorama*, Collins 1961, pp. 112f.
5. Exod. 3.14.
6. See J. L. Mackie, 'Evil and Omnipotence', *Mind* 64, 1955, p. 210; J. Hick, *Philosophy of Religion*, Prentice-Hall 1963, pp. 42f.
7. See Aquinas, *Summa contra Gentiles* III, ch. 65.
8. Augustine, *Confessions* I, I.
9. See, for example, M. Ruse, *The Philosophy of Biology*, Hutchinson 1973, pp. 176f.
10. W. Sherlock, *Discourse concerning Divine Providence*, London 1694, p. 35.
11. Moses Maimonides (ben Maimon), *The Guide of the Perplexed*, translated by S. Pines, University of Chicago Press 1963, III, 17 (the book was originally written in Arabic).
12. Ibid., III, 24.
13. Ibid., III, 17, cf. also III, 18, 51.
14. See W. T. Davison, 'Providence', *Encyclopaedia of Religion and Ethics* 10 edited by J. Hastings, T. & T. Clark 1918, pp. 415–20.
15. I Kings 18.
16. *Confessions*, V, VII, VIII and XIII; VI, I; cf. *De ordine* I, 5, 14.
17. W. T. Davison, op. cit., p. 419.
18. Confessions, VII, VIII.
19. Sherlock, op. cit., p. 24.
20. Ibid., pp. 47f.
21. Ibid., pp. 183f.
22. Sherlock's view is not identical to universal providence, for the latter would include the total control of man's inner thoughts.
23. See I. Stewart, 'The Seven Elementary Catastrophes', *New Scientist* 68, 20 November 1975.

24. M. Dibelius, *Paul*, edited by W. G. Kümmel, Longmans 1953, ch. 4.

25. *ST* 1a, q. 114 a. 4. Cf. 1a, q. 110, a. 4 and 2, 2ae q. 178, a. 1. Translations from the *Summa Theologiae* are from the Blackfriars edition, edited by T. Gilbey and others, London 1964ff.

26. *ST* 1a, q. 105 a. 7.

27. E.g. *ST* 1a, q. 22, a. 3 and q. 105, a. 5.

28. E.g., John Hick, op. cit., p. 39.

29. Mark 6.37f.

30. The history of hypnotism, especially since the time of F. A. Mesmer (1734–1815), is a classic example of the expansion of scientific thought in order to take account of an area of human experience that had been under suspicion.

31. David Hume, *Enquiry concerning Human Understanding*, section 10.

32. C. S. Lewis, *Miracles*, Collins 1960, pp. 63f. In an appendix, Lewis rejects the notion of a providence that is identified neither with miracle nor with the ordinary running of nature. It will be evident that I do not agree with Lewis here.

33. D. D. Raphael, *Problems of Political Philosophy*, Pall Mall Press 1970, pp. 12f.

34. John 11.1–44.

35. By 'public' in this context I do not mean that the events must be open to investigation by all, like the 'public' and repeatable observations made in science, but that they could, in principle, be witnessed by the physical senses of a number of people.

36. Mark 7.36.

37. John Macquarrie, *Principles of Christian Theology*, SCM Press 1966, p. 228.

38. W. Paley, *View of the Evidences of Christianity*, 1794.

39. I. Kant, *Critique of Pure Reason*, Transcendental Dialectic, Book II, ch. 3, section VI.

40. E.g. in C. H. Powell, *Secrets of Answered Prayer*, Arthur James 1958, pp. 68f.

41. *De divinatione* II, 59. See also R. Harvie, in A. Hardy, R. Harvie and A. Koestler, *The Challenge of Chance*, Hutchinson 1973, p. 126.

42. Macgibbon and Kee 1966.

43. E.g. I. Stevenson, *Journal of the American Society for Psychical Research* 61, 3, July 1967, pp. 254f.; R. G. Medhurst, *Journal of the Society for Psychical Research* 44, 735, March 1968, pp. 217f.; C. Honorton, *The Journal of Parapsychology* 31, 1, March 1967, pp. 76f.

44. Dietrich Bonhoeffer, *Letters and Papers from Prison. An Abridged Edition*, SCM Press 1981, p. 133. Cf. II Cor. 12.9; 13.4

45. See his *The Biology of God*, Jonathan Cape 1975, p. 230.

46. Habakkuk 3.17f.; cf. Job 13.15; Micah 7.7.

47. In *The Reasonableness of Christianity*, 1695, Locke describes virtue as 'much the best bargain because of the fact of eternal life', *Works*, London 1823, Vol. 7, pp. 150f. Paley had a similar view.

48. R. B. Braithwaite, *An Empiricist's View of the Nature of Religious Belief*, Cambridge University Press 1955, especially pp. 11, 16.

49. I Corinthians 10.13.

50. *Confessions* VII, V; cf. I and III.

51. *ST* 1a, q. 14, a. 7.

52. *ST* 1a, q. 10 a. 1; cf. q. 9. a. 1f.

53. *ST* 1a, q. 14 a. 13.

54. *ST* 1a, q. 20 a. 1.

55. *Confessions*, XI, XIIf.

56. Anselm, *Proslogion*.

57. E.g. Prov. 8.22f.; Isa. 55.11; Wisdom 1.7; 7.22f.; 8.1–5; 9.17; Ecclus. 24.1–9.

58. Job 42.3.

59. A. N. Whitehead, *Process and Reality* (1929), Harper and Row 1960, p. 532, cf. p. 377. See also I. G. Barbour, *Issues in Science and Religion*, SCM Press 1966, pp. 440–4, for a useful summary of Whitehead's views.

Chapter II The Historical Background

1. Wisdom 14.3; 17.2.

2. Amos 3.6.

3. E. R. Dodds, *The Greeks and the Irrational*, University of California Press (1951) 1973, pp. 7, 30f.

4. E.g. Isa. 1.16–20; Jer. 21.8.

5. Jer. 31.29–31; Ezek. 18.2–4.

6. Jer. 18.6.

7. Gen. 1; 2.

8. Cf. Jer. 31.35; Job 38–41.

9. Exod. 14.21.

10. Exod. 15.8; cf. Pss. 33.7; 78.13.

11. Judg. 6.36f.

12. Acts 24.2.

13. Matt. 5.45.

14. Matt. 10.29.

15. Matt. 11.4.

16. Mark 7.36.

17. John 2.11.

18. Matt. 18.12; cf. 12.11; Luke 15.8.

19. Mark 14.36.

20. Aristoxemus, *Elements of Harmony* II, 30f.; Plato, *Letters*, 2.314; 7.341f.

21. *Letters*, 2.312e–313a; 6.323d.

22. *Republic*, 508.

23. *Republic*, 514f.

24. *Symposium*, 186–8.

25. *Symposium*, 201–12.

26. G. E. R. Lloyd, *Aristotle: The Growth and Structure of His Thought*, Cambridge University Press 1968, pp. 156f.

27. *Nichomachean Ethics*, 1177b, 1178b.

28. *Nichomachean Ethics*, 1159a.

29. *Metaphysics*, 1074b, 1072b, cf. *Nichomachean Ethics*, 1154b.

30. *Physics*, 198a.

31. *Metaphysics*, 996b, cf. *Physics*, 194b–195a.

32. See W. A. Wallace, *Causality and Scientific Explanation*, University of Michigan Press 1972, Vol. 1, p. 18.

33. *Physics*, 195b.

34. See G. E. R. Lloyd, *Aristotle*, pp. 160f.

35. *Metaphysics*, 1072a–b.

36. *Physics*, 242a, cf. Aquinas' 'first way', *ST* 1a, q. 2, a. 3. The argument from motion was not invented by Aristotle. A version of it is found in Plato, *Laws* X, 893b–895b.

37. *Metaphysics*, 1074b (translated by R. Hope).

38. David Hume, *Dialogues concerning Natural Religion*, Part 2.

39. Christopher Butler, in *The Truth of God Incarnate*, edited by Michael Green, Hodder and Stoughton 1977, p. 93.

40. E. H. Gilson, 'Saint Thomas Aquinas', *Proceedings of the British Academy*, Vol. 21, 1935.

41. *De Potentia* III, 7c. Quoted by I. G. Barbour, *Issues in Science and Religion*, SCM Press 1966, p. 426.

42. *Summa contra Gentiles*, III, ch. 29.

43. *ST* 1a, q. 105, a. 5, cf. q. 22, a. 3; q. 103, a. 6; q. 104, a. 2.

44. *Commentary on Aristotle's Physics*, translated by R. J. Blackwell, R. J. Spath, W. E. Thirlkell, Yale University Press 1963, II, 185, at p. 91 (referring to 195a).

45. Ibid., II, 250 at p. 116 (referring to 198b).

46. *ST* 1a, q. 105, a. 5.

47. *ST* 1a q. 22, a. 1.

48. *ST* 1a, q. 22, aa. 1 and 3.

49. *ST* 1a, q. 105, aa. 6–7, and see Introduction, section 2, 6.

50. *ST* 1a, q. 105, a. 5.

51. Calvin, *Institutes*, translated by H. Beveridge, I, XVI, 5, cf. the whole of sections XVI–XVIII.

52. R. Hooker, *Ecclesiastical Polity* (1593), Book 1.

53. John Wesley, *Works*, ed. T. Jackson, London [11]1856, Vol. VI, pp. 299–301, cf. *Letters*, ed. J. Telford, Epworth Press 1931, Vol. II, p. 379.

54. *De augmentis scientiarium* 3, 5, quoted by W. A. Wallace, *Causality and Scientific Explanation* (n. 32 above), Vol. 2, p. 85.

55. *Novum Organum* 2, 2; *De augmentis scientiarium* 3, 4.

56. W. A. Wallace, op. cit., Vol. 1, p. 189.

57. *Principles of Philosophy* I, no. 28.

58. *De corpore*, chapter 10, 7.

59. I. G. Barbour, *Issues in Science and Religion*, SCM Press 1966, p. 35.

60. Ibid., p. 36.

61. Compare John Lilburne, *An Answer to Nine Arguments* (1638), and *Come out of her my people* (1639), with his *The Legal Fundamentall Liberties of the People of England* (1649) and other later tracts.

62. *Two Treatises of Government* (1690). The first is an attack on Robert Filmer's use of the Bible to support the doctrine of the divine right of kings, the second grounds Locke's own theory in what he claims to be reason, especially in chs. 6 and 7.

63. *The True Intellectual System of the Universe*, London 1678, Book. 1, ch. 3, section 37, p. 147.

64. Ibid., p. 148.

65. Ibid., p. 155.

66. Ibid., p. 150.

Chapter III   Analogies for Divine Action

1. Ps. 103.13 (while I have generally used RSV for biblical quotations, because of the familiarity of the language, I have retained the translation of the Psalms from the *Book of Common Prayer*).

2. *Summa contra Gentiles* I, ch. 34, cf. ST 1a, q. 13 a. 5.

3. See *ST* 1a, q. 13 a. 6, and *Summa contra Gentiles* I, chs. 28–34.

4. I Cor. 13.12.

5. Ps. 84.11.

6. Rev. 1.16.

7. E.g. Deut. 4.19.

8. E.g. Ps. 27.1; Isa. 60.20.

9. Ps. 36.9.

10. Ps. 139.10f.

11. *The English Hymnal*, no. 404.

12. E.g. I Kings 18.45.

13. E.g. Gen. 6.17.

14. E.g. Isa. 57.15f.

15. Gen. 1.2.

16. Judg. 14.19.

17. Ps. 139.7.

18. John 3.8.

19. 'Idea for a Universal History from a Cosmopolitan Point of View', in *On History*, ed. L. W. Beck, Bobbs-Merrill, New York 1963, p. 11.

20. I Cor. 15.41.

21. *ST* 1a, q. 46, a. 2.

22. According to Kant, the real self is bound neither by space nor by time. However, while I am convinced that on a Christian view the 'person' is not in space in the way in which physical objects are, I want to leave open the question of whether he is necessarily in time. It may be the case that being subject to temporal succession is a precondition of any personal life.

23. *Leviathan*, ch. 6.

24. H. D. Lewis, *The Elusive Mind*, Allen and Unwin 1969, especially ch. 11; and., *The Self and Immortality*, Macmillan 1973, chs. 2–4.
25. J. Locke, *Essay concerning Human Understanding*, Book 2, Ch. 21; T. Reid, *Essays on the Intellectual Powers of Man*, 6, 5, 6.
26. *Phaedo*, 99.
27. P. J. Donovan, *A Philosophical Analysis of the Doctrine of Providence*, Oxford DPhil. thesis 1971, pp. 212, 232.
28. Job 38.
29. Ps. 104.2.
30. Cf. Thomas Reid, *Essays on the Intellectual Powers of Man*, 1, 4 (Of analogy).
31. Sherlock, op. cit., pp. 35f.

Chapter IV   Providence in the Order of Nature

1. See P. J. Donovan, *Philosophical Analysis* (ch. 3 n. 27 above), pp. 235, 250.
2. See for example I. G. Barbour, op. cit., pp. 383–6, 417f., 458.
3. Amos 4.7.
4. R. Harré and E. H. Madden, *Causal Powers*, Blackwell 1975.
5. W. Sherlock, op. cit., p. 37.
6. C. A. Coulson, *Science and Christian Belief*, Oxford University Press 1955, p. 22.
7. Coulson, op. cit., p. 38.
8. W. G. Pollard, *Chance and Providence*, Scribner, New York 1958.
9. Pollard, op. cit., pp. 38, 43.
10. Ibid., p. 73.
11. Ibid., p. 71.
12. Ibid., p. 78.
13. Ibid., p. 86.
14. E.g. ibid., pp. 106f.
15. Ibid., pp. 96f., 122f; cf. I. G. Barbour, op. cit., p. 429.
16. E.g. Mark 6.48.
17. Acts 27.7f.
18. Mark 4.39.
19. Rom. 8.22f.
20. R. Bultmann, *Jesus Christ and Mythology*, SCM Press 1960.
21. Bultmann, op. cit., pp. 37f., 65.
22. Ibid., p. 68.
23. Included in C. G. Jung, *The Interpretation of Nature and the Psyche*, Routledge and Kegan Paul 1955.
24. See A. Koestler, *The Roots of Coincidence*, Hutchinson 1972, pp. 83–7.
25. C. G. Jung, op. cit., pp. 14, 95.
26. Ibid., p. 144.
27. E.g. ibid., p. 123.
28. See Koestler, op. cit., pp. 88–90.
29. Ibid., p. 98.

Notes

Notes173

30. John Beloff, in *Journal of the Society for Psychical Research* 49, no. 773, September 1977.

31. Ibid., p. 576.

32. Ibid., pp. 577, 582.

33. Karl Heim, *Christian Faith and Natural Science*, SCM Press 1953.

34. Martin Buber, *I and Thou*, T. and T. Clark 1937.

35. See, for example, A. N. Whitehead, *Process and Reality*, Harper and Row 1960, p. 75.

36. Charles Hartshorne, *The Divine Relativity*, Yale University Press 1948, p. 17.

37. Hartshorne, op. cit., pp. 20, 45f.; cf. id., *The Logic of Perfection*, Open Court Publishing Co., LaSalle, Illinois 1962.

38. Barbour, op. cit., p. 445.

39. I. Kant, *Critique of Pure Reason*, Transcendental Dialectic, Book III, ch. 3, section VII.

40. H. Grotius, *De jure belli ac pacis*, translated by F. W. Kelsey and others, Oxford 1913–27, I, 1, X, 5; II, 11, IV, 1.

41. *ST* 1a, q. 23, especially a. 5.

42. The problem centres on the proper interpretation of Paul in Rom. 8.29f.; Eph. 1.5, 11. Liberal theologians tend to interpret *proorizo*, the word translated as 'predestinate', to refer to the Christian experience of grace, whereby, looking back at how the Christian came to be what he is, in so far as this is good, he stresses the grace of God in seeking him out and choosing him, and without which he would have been lost. This leaves open the questions of how far the Christian's own will had also to be active, and how far God has influenced others who have not as yet responded. See, for example, C. H. Dodd's comments on the former passage in *The Epistle to the Romans*, Hodder and Stoughton 1932.

43. See Dorothy L. Sayers, *The Mind of the Maker*, Methuen 1941, for a far-reaching use of this analogy, though here the emphasis is more on the freedom open to the creative artist, while I have stressed the limitations imposed by the medium.

44. F. J. Ayala, 'Teleological Explanations in Evolutionary Biology', *Philosophy of Science* 37, 1970, p. 1. Cf. M. Ruse, op. cit., p. 196.

45. E.g. L. Wright, *Teleological Explanations*, University of California Press 1976, and A. Woodfield, *Teleology*, Cambridge University Press 1976.

46. Woodfield, op. cit., pp. 218f.

47. Charles Raven, *Natural Religion and Christian Theology*, Cambridge University Press 1953, Vol. 2, pp. 131–44; cf. Rom. 1.19f.

48. P. Lecompte du Nouy, *Human Destiny*, Longmans Green, New York 1947, p. 36.

49. E. E. Harris, *The Foundations of Metaphysics in Science*, Allen and Unwin 1965, p. 259.

50. E.g. T. Dobzhansky, *The Biology of Ultimate Concern*, Rapp and Whiting 1969; 'The reality is, however, more complex and more interesting than the chance vs. design dichotomy suggests' (p. 125).

51. L. J. Henderson, *The Fitness of the Environment*, Macmillan, New York 1913.

52. C. F. A. Pantin, in *Biology and Personality*, ed. I. T. Ramsey, Blackwell 1965, p. 102, cf. pp. 94, 100, 104.

53. Note the reference to 'the wider teleology' in *Philosophical Theology*, Cambridge University Press 1928, 1930, Vol. 2, p. 79.

Chapter V Providence and Human Nature

1. T. Dobzhansky, op. cit., p. 43: 'Stated most simply, the phenomena of the inorganic, organic and human levels are subject to different laws peculiar to those levels.' However, Dobzhansky does not commit himself to the final irreducibility of the laws of one level to those of another.

2. C. G. Hempel, *Philosophy of Natural Science*, Prentice-Hall 1966, pp. 104f.; see also C. Taylor, *The Explanation of Behavior*, Routledge and Kegan Paul 1964, who argues against reductionism. See also L. Wright, op. cit., pp. 66f., and M. Ruse, op. cit., pp. 196, 213.

3. B. F. Skinner, *Science and Human Behaviour*, Macmillan, New York 1966, p. 6.

4. Ibid., p. 17.

5. Ibid., pp. 283–5 (the emphasis is his).

6. G. Ryle, *The Concept of Mind*, Hutchinson 1949.

7. See Chapter III, section 6.

8. Iris Murdoch, *The Sovereignty of Good*, Routledge and Kegan Paul 1970, pp. 17f.

9. W. Sherlock, op. cit., p. 51.

10. Ibid., p. 53.

11. Ibid., p. 49.

12. Ibid., p. 50.

13. See Chapter I, section 2 subsection 5.

14. *Apology*, 28a; *Republic*, 361 and 364 (in the *Republic*, where the prediction is more explicit, it is in fact made by Plato's brothers).

15. John 6.64.

16. *ST* 1a, q. 14, a. 13 ad 3.

17. *De consolatione* V, VI, 66–72 (Loeb Classical Library).

18. Luke 4.22.

19. Hosea 2.19; cf. Ps. 36.7; Isa. 63.7.

20. E.g. Rom. 3.22.

21. Rom. 5.8.

22. E.g. Rom. 3.24.

23. Eph. 2.8.

24. See, for example, R. Garrigou-Lagrange, *Grace*, Herder 1952.

25. *ST* 1a, q. 22, a. 4. The double negative (in both text and translation) is misleading.

26. II Cor. 6.1.

27. *Phaedrus*, 246.

28. I am referring here to memory of specific facts and events. In another sense, memory may be required in order to give substance to the

dispositions, or to the relationships that I shall later claim to be in part constitutive of the person. Interestingly, those who believe in reincarnation normally do not regard memories of the alleged past lives as essential to the claim that there is a continuity of the person, though where such memories appear to be present, this is certainly used as evidence for the belief.

29. John 12.24.

30. J. W. Oman, *Grace and Personality*, Cambridge University Press ⁴1931. See pp. 66, 88, for the distinction between individuals and persons.

31. Acts 27.

32. *ST* 1, 2ae, q. 109, aa 2, 4.

33. John 1.1–14.

34. Matt. 25.31–40.

35. John 12.32.

36. See G. E. H. Aulen, *Christus Victor*, SPCK 1931, pp. 112–14.

37. Ibid., pp. 100f. (on Anselm) and 117f. (on Luther).

38. Rom. 6.3–8.

39. E.g. II Cor. 5.17; Gal. 6.15; Rom. 12.4f.; Eph. 2.15f.; II Cor. 1.7; I Peter 4.13; I Cor. 10.17.

40. See also Chapter I, sections 2, 6, and section 4.

41. *The Myth of God Incarnate*, edited by John Hick, SCM Press 1977.

42. Col. 1.15; cf. 2.9 and Heb. 1.3.

43. J. L. Mackie, 'Evil and Omnipotence', *Mind* 64, 1955, p. 209.

44. *Ethics*, 1137a § 31–1138a.

45. Strictly, not in the *Confession*, but in the *Shorter Catechism* (1648), question 1.

46. Matt. 6.13.

47. Luke 22.42.

48. I Cor. 10.13; II Cor. 12.9. See also A. M. Farrer, *Love Almighty and Ills Unlimited*, Collins 1962.

Chapter VI Providence and History

1. R. G. Collingwood, *The Idea of History*, Clarendon Press 1946, pp. 46f.

2. E.g. Ps. 78.12.

3. Josh. 7.4f.

4. *Metaphysics*, 980a.

5. While I am stressing here the role of general providence in the interpretation of large-scale religious movements, I do not wish to deny that the prophets may have had individual experiences which were the result of special providence.

6. Exod. 3.11; 4.1, 10, 13.

7. Luke 1.38.

8. Collingwood, op. cit., pp. 17–19.

9. E.g. Amos 2.6f.

10. Isa. 42.6, cf. 60.3.

11. Isa. 53.

12. See, for example II Kings 17–19 and 23.27; also Isa. 45.1.
13. See Collingwood, op. cit., pp. 20f., 49–52, and K. Löwith, *Meaning in History*, University of Chicago Press 1949, Introduction and pp. 44f.
14. Isa. 42.1.
15. Rom. 1.18; 11.21.
16. *Republic*, 352.
17. G. Vico, *The New Science*, revised translation of the third edition (1744) by T. G. Bergin and M. H. Fisch, Cornell University Press 1963, sections 54, 165f., 172, 396.
18. Ibid., section 313.
19. Section 31.
20. Sections 344 and M 9, cf. 1106.
21. Sections 1089–94, cf. 348, 1096.
22. Section 1106.
23. Section 342.
24. Section 348, cf. 342.
25. See K. Löwith, op. cit., p. 123.
26. G. W. F. Hegel, *The Philosophy of History*, translated J. Sibree, Dover Publications 1956, pp. 13f.
27. Marx does not claim that there will be no social evolution after the introduction of true communism, and in one of his philosophical manuscripts he writes, 'communism is not itself the goal of human development' (See Erich Fromm, *Marx's Concept of Man*, F. Ungar Publishing Co, New York 1966, which contains T. B. Bottomore's translation of Marx's *Economic and Philosophical Manuscripts*. The quotation is on p. 140.) However, after the arrival of true communism there will be no more class struggle and consequently no more revolutions. In an important sense the historical process will have come to an end.
28. Reinhold Niebuhr, *Faith and History*, Nisbet 1949, esp. ch. 13.
29. Compare Exod. 20.5 with Jer. 31.29f.
30. The use of the word 'discovery' at this point is somewhat question-begging. I am in fact expressing a point of view rather than advancing an argument. A more adequate treatment of the subject would need to present arguments to support the view that the language of discovery is appropriate for the acceptance of certain moral values.
31. S. Freud, *Moses and Monotheism*, Hogarth Press 1939.
32. In some contexts 'revelation' refers to the spiritual truths that are alleged to be disclosed, either through writings, or by direct communication with man: in others it refers to events that are said to be revelatory, as when the incarnation is said to be a revelation of God's love. In a third type of context, the reference is to a body of writings which is claimed either to reveal truth directly or to describe significant and revelatory events. The result is that there are at least three senses of the word 'revelation'.

Chapter VII   The Rational Evaluation of the Concept of
Providence

1. See F. Engels, 'Letter to Starkenburg', reprinted in *Reader in Marxist Philosophy*, ed. H. Selsam and H. Martel, International Publishers, New York 1963, pp. 201–3, cf. pp. 190, 193.

2. M. Polanyi, *Science, Faith and Society*, University of Chicago Press 1946, ch. 2, especially pp. 50–4.

3. I Cor. 13.12; Rom. 8.24f.; cf. Heb. 11.1

4. E.g. the references just above. The term 'Christian agnostic' is now gaining acceptance, though it would have seemed odd to former generations.

5. R. W. Hepburn, *Christianity and Paradox* (1958), Pegasus, New York 1968, pp. 44–7, 205–8.

6. M. Tindal, *Christianity as Old as Creation*, London 1730. Note pp. 4–6 on the universality of natural revelation.

7. 'This is the Spirit that Beauty must ever induce, wonderment and a delicious trouble, longing and love and a troubling that is all delight. For the unseen all this may be felt as for the seen; and this the Souls feel for it, every Soul in some degree, but those the more deeply that are the more truly apt to this higher love.' (Plotinus, *The Enneads*, translated by S. MacKenna, Faber ⁴1969, 5, 8, 4, cf. 1, 6 and 5, 8 passim).

8. For an introduction to Sankara's thought see Y. K. Menon and R. F. Allen, *The Pure Principle*, Michigan State University Press 1960.

9. Strictly speaking, not all adjectives that are applied to God are applied to God as the prime analogue. For example, when God is called 'jealous' in the Old Testament it would be absurd to say that we can learn what 'true' jealousy is from God. In such cases the prime analogue is human, and the word is not applied strictly to God.

10. John 3.3; Eph. 4.22; Col. 3.9.

11. For the Christian, man is in a crucial sense dependent on God, so that the notion of 'friendship' with God refers to only one aspect of man's relationship. However, there has been a tendency to neglect the kind of 'independence' that providence appears to thrust upon man.

12. Blaise Pascal, *Pensées*, translated by W. F. Trotter, Dent 1931, no. 233, pp. 66–8.

13. William James, *The Will to Believe and Other Essays in Popular Philosophy*, Longman, New York 1897.

14. Phil. 2.11; cf. Rom. 10.9; Acts 8.16; 10.48; 19.5.

15. Eph. 1.13.

16. I Peter 3.15.

17. Dietrich Bonhoeffer, *Letters and Papers from Prison. An Abridged Edition*, SCM Press 1981, pp. 129f. In this context Bonhoeffer quotes Matt. 8.17. The Latin quotation is a reference to Grotius' famous claim that there would be a natural (moral) law of a kind, even if there were no God (*De jure belli ac pacis*, Prolegomena, section 11).

18. Bonhoeffer, op. cit., p. 91.

19. The term 'fundamentalism' is used in different senses. The most

common usage refers to the belief that the scriptures (of the Christian or any other tradition) are verbally inspired, so that there can be no error except for false copying of the original text, or false translation. In this usage there is no need for the fundamentalist to believe that Adam was created in an instant of time, since God might perfectly well have dictated portions of Genesis with the intent that they should be used as myth or parable. In practice, however, most of those who call themselves 'fundamentalists' tend to believe both in the verbal inspiration and in the literal history of Genesis.

20. See the Introduction, section 4.

21. *Westminster Confession* (1647), chs. 3 and 9.

22. *ST* 1a, q. 2 a. 3.

23. First, there is the possibility that there might be increasing evidence that the order of nature was totally closed and predictable. Second, further evidence might increasingly question the reality of human freedom. Third, human nature might be found not to have the openness that I claimed to be a precondition of the possibility of grace. Fourth, history might seem to be more and more a meaningless saga of woe. Fifth, historical research might cast doubt on some crucial events, at least so far as Christianity is concerned, or it might indicate that Jesus was less than morally perfect (see the last note). Sixth, and most importantly, there is the possibility (and frequent actuality) of a negative evaluation of the personal hypothesis discussed in the introduction.

24. See the introduction to the edition of Pascal's *Pensées* referred to above (n. 12), p. XII.

25. I. Kant, *Critique of Practical Reason*, Part I, Book II, ch. 2, sections 4–6.

26. Hepburn, op. cit., p. 146.

27. The point here must be stated with care. Building on a position made famous by Plato in his *Euthyphro* (9e–11b), the mainstream Christian tradition has always claimed that God commands what is good, not that good simply is what God commands, for otherwise it would be meaningless to claim that God is good. (However, whereas Plato placed the Good above the gods, Christians do not place the Good above God; rather, they claim that Good is in some way identical with his nature. God is not controlled by something higher than himself, but his will is conditioned by his nature, so that it is inconceivable that he should will other than the good.) Similarly, since the Christian believes that Jesus is the image of God, he believes that all his commandments would be good, but it is not his commanding of them that *makes* them good. In consequence, if the Christian were to find that Jesus had made some demands that were in inescapable conflict with his basic moral convictions (perhaps in some newly discovered manuscripts), and if he were to be consistent with the mainstream tradition, he would be bound to doubt whether Jesus really were the image of God after all. Thus part of what it means to believe that Jesus is the image of God is the belief that no such evidence will be forthcoming. Appropriately, on many occasions Jesus seems to have backed away from being treated as an infallible source.

When asked for an answer to a puzzle he frequently asked another question that challenged the questioner to work things out for himself.

Index